CIRCUS

•

PARABLE

•

CONSTRUCTION

Three One-Act Plays

CIRCUS

•

PARABLE

•

CONSTRUCTION

Three One-Act Plays
by RALPH STONE

THE BETHANY PRESS • ST. LOUIS

CONTENTS

INTRODUCTION

Circus, Parable, and *Construction* are three one-act plays which were written especially for presentation at the Second Quadrennial Assembly of International Christian Women's Fellowship, July 19-23, 1961. These plays lift up the decisions which confront modern-day individuals in the areas of vocation, stewardship, and outreach. Each play uses a unique dramatic vehicle to convey its message—a circus, a fantasy of the imagination, and the misty flats of Here-and-Now.

In *Circus,* young Anna Lu comes upon Life in the form of a circus. She is confronted with the many roles that a woman-to-be may assume, the demands and opportunities which accompany each role. She suddenly becomes aware of the essential question: What will she do in the Circus of Life? She faces the necessity of making her own choice, aware that others may advise, suggest, and even pressure her, but it is she who must ultimately decide.

History has held royalty accountable for what it did with what it was privileged to hold—stewardship, in a word. The question of who we are and what we do with that which we hold is the one on which *Parable* is based. Queen Nancy finds herself confronted with the necessity to choose from the many points of view thrust upon her. Only she can choose the course of action she must follow in being a wise stewardess.

In the misty flats of Here-and-Now, ten people find themselves surrounded by tools and materials with which to build something, they know not what. They grow fearful, suspicious, and argumentative as they wait. When they become aware of unknown and unseen forces surrounding them, they decide to construct a wall for protection. *Construction* focuses on the eruptions of apprehen-

9

sion and fear which dictate the actions of those who will not listen
to The Builder as he speaks of human love and divine intention.

These plays were written and produced at the Quadrennial Assembly by the capable young Disciple dramatist, Ralph Stone. Mr.
Stone is one of the most outstanding and creative religious drama-
tists on the American Protestant church scene today. He was ably
assisted in these productions by his wife, Jan, by Emmet Smith,
professor of organ at Texas Christian University, and by the Texas
Players, a dramatics group of University Christian Church, Fort
Worth, formed especially for this occasion.

The Formal Program Committee of the Second Quadrennial Assembly is deeply indebted to Mr. Stone, his cast, and crew for the
impact which these daily dramatic presentations made upon the
more than 3,000 delegates to the Assembly.

Martha W. Faw, Staff Advisor
Formal Program Committee
Second Quadrennial Assembly

September, 1961

CIRCUS

Cast of Characters

ANNA LU—a young lady emerging from adolescence into adult womanhood, still full of curiosity, energy, and imagination. She wears a big straw hat, pigtails, and a full skirt. She swings her purse with abandon as she ventures into Life.

CLOWN—a young man behind the grease paint of a clown who has much support to offer but few words. He represents all the support that comes to a person making a decision, but still retains the mask or role which he has chosen for himself.

BALLADEER—the person of continuity for this play. He starts the program with his ballad, interjects verses from time to time, and draws the conclusion of the play in the same manner.

PUPPETS—three actors who are attached with strings to the "other" that directs them. They are animated only when other-directed. They are representative of aimless living, other-directed living, and are made to appear alive and happy though empty inside.

BAREBACK RIDER—an actress who rides a bicycle in a circle constantly, stopping only to speak of her routine life that at least is kept filled. The work-a-day world of "doing" things is reflected in this Circus character.

DIVA—an artist of the trapeze, she comes in on the shoulders of several males. She represents the image of the female in our culture best characterized by Hollywood "blonds." She is the woman as sexually symbolized in our society.

TIGHTROPE WALKER—a lady of social-climbing tendencies who is going to work her way to the top in whatever field she chooses. She is success-conscious to the point of absurdity.

ANIMAL TRAINER—a lady who cracks the whip while the trained animals perform. She achieves her ends in various ways, not to exclude tears if necessary. "Mom-ism" is the characteristic of this performer.

RINGMASTER—this gentleman serves to call attention to the next big attraction. He gives some insights to ANNA LU from time to time as she observes the roles that appear before her.

SEVERAL OTHERS for nonspeaking roles as indicated in the script.

It should be noted that all of the roles depicted in this play are not without merit. For purposes of this drama, however, they are given more emphasis than is normally the case in order to draw out dramatic and discussional values.

About this play

Emerging from immaturity into maturity, ANNA LU comes upon Life in the form of a circus. She is confronted, perhaps for the first time in a real sense, with the task of assuming responsibility for her own life. She gazes upon the wonders of the exciting world about her, seeing the many roles that a woman-to-be can assume, demands placed upon her, and opportunities that can be seized. Each role in turn confronts ANNA LU who finds some solace in the friendship of a CLOWN who helps her see what Life has to offer her, and what lies beyond the surface. Whirling in the maze of possibilities ANNA LU is suddenly aware of the essential question: What will she do in the Circus of Life? Even in turning to her friend, the CLOWN, she is without comfort, for he reminds her that his face is a false one and that he fulfills the role he has chosen for himself, and she must now choose her own. He urges only that she make a choice of integrity in which she gives full consideration to what she has to offer to Life—what she ought to give to Life. The curtain falls as ANNA LU is becoming aware of what it means to be a mature woman with a contribution to make to Life, and what great need there is for a perspective from which to view Life and make a decision.

The Setting

The stage is made to look a little like a Circus with a center ring for performers; a platform with bright stripes to one side; some ropes, flags, and banners hanging above. A gilded ladder is suspended in the ring. It is used by the TIGHTROPE WALKER.

At the beginning of the play the curtain is closed and the BALLADEER is standing in front of it. When it opens, ANNA LU is the only one visible, and she moves across the stage with a single spot following her. At the extreme L of the stage is a large poster advertising the Circus of Life. This she reads with enthusiasm, and through it the CLOWN jumps as the lights suddenly reveal the full stage. The poster is then removed.

BALLADEER: *(in front of the curtain)* Good morning, ladies. For our drama this morning I am to be your host, or narrator, or whatever you may wish to call me. And you may suspect that I will tell the story in song. *(Seats himself on a stool DR)* Creeping back into our culture is the ballad. Stories have been told in this manner for centuries and we Americans are once more discovering them. Usually ballads sung today are very old. They were new at one time, however, and this is the justification for what we are about to do. We plan to sing a modern-day ballad, "The Ballad of Anna Lu."

(Curtain opens revealing Anna Lu)

"The Ballad of Anna Lu"

Stanza 1

Oh, tell us true, Pretty Anna Lu,
How strange our world must seem,
With your flaxen hair and your eyes of blue,
And the fun that a little girl schemes.

(Music for "The Ballad of Anna Lu" is found on page 35)

(speaking) The world of Anna Lu was very small when she was a little girl—it was filled with wonders and surprises, a few hurts and bruises, but lots of adventure. It was not always easy to be a little girl in a big world, but it was usually fun, and each new day brought a new discovery to Anna Lu.

(During this preceding statement, ANNA LU has been skipping rope and playing like a small girl—laughing, jumping, making faces.)

(Repeat Stanza 1)

BALLADEER: Anna Lu grew up—or growed up—as she said it. She learned her letters, learned her manners, and learned to get along with boys. Now boys are not always easy to get along with, especially when you have long pigtails and a peppy spirit. But like everything else in your young life you learn how to deal with the situation. Anna Lu learned and she grew, and she became a young lady.

(During this ANNA LU pretends to have a tussle with a boy who pulls her pigtails, at first being very tomboyish about

*it, then taking on the attitude of some refinement as a
young lady.)*

(Repeat Stanza 1)

Anna Lu grew right up into a teen-age girl, went away to school,
and was about to enter into the full-time business of being a lady
when she discovered that her world was much bigger than she had
imagined for so many years. She awoke suddenly to discover that
her life was very much in her hands, and she was responsible for it.
And with this awareness, Anna Lu was about to embark upon the
Venture of Life—mature, responsible life. And she had to make
decisions about how she would live it.

> *(During this* ANNA LU *moves to the Circus of Life poster
> and reads it. She is licking a large lollipop which she finally
> discards. Just at the end of the refrain she is startled as the
> CLOWN jumps through the sign, the lights come up full on
> the stage, and the Circus set is revealed with* RINGMASTER,
> *animals, and performers.)*

(Repeat Stanza 1)

> *(There is musical accompaniment as the circus performers
> parade and the animals are displayed. The* RINGMASTER *is
> calling, "Hurry, hurry! Step right this way, ladies and gen-
> tlemen." This continues for a few moments as* ANNA LU
> *and the* CLOWN *enjoy the excitement. The lights reduce to
> a spot on the* RINGMASTER, *the music stops, and the circus
> performers retire to the wings.* ANNA LU *and her friend,
> the* CLOWN, *stand at the edge of the light.)*

RINGMASTER: Ladies and gentlemen, boys and girls, welcome to the
Circus of Life. The most significant, gigantic, stupendous ex-
travaganza ever assembled before the eyes of people anywhere.
Here you will witness the daring deeds that give zest to living;
you will see for yourself those mysterious freaks of nature; you
will thrill to the precision of trained man and beast alike. This
is the Circus of Life, the greatest of all shows, the show above
all shows. *(slight pause)* For this performance today we have
among the distinguished guests in our audience, Miss Anna Lu,
a young lady of twenty years who is here to embark upon her adventure in Life. Ladies and gentlemen, allow me to present to
you our distinguished guest, Miss Anna Lu!

*(The spotlight finds her on the edge of the circle, and the
ringmaster escorts her and her friend, the* CLOWN, *to the
center ring of light.)*

RINGMASTER: Welcome, Miss Anna Lu, to the Circus of Life.

ANNA LU: Thank you, Mr. Ringmaster, thank you very much. I
am so excited that I hardly know what to say. I have always
wanted to come to the Circus and see what it is like, and now
that I'm here, I am too excited to breathe.

RINGMASTER: My dear young lady, you are not only at the Circus
of Life, but you are being invited now to come take part. This
is the unique and outstanding feature of our great show—you
cannot be a spectator for long, or the circus will pass you by.
And so we are inviting you to come now and take part.

ANNA LU: Take part—become a part of the Circus! I never
dreamed—oh, this is wonderful. (*Turns to the* CLOWN) Isn't this
wonderful, Mr. Clown? Now I can be in the show just like you—
maybe I can even be a clown like you. Oh, this is wonderful.
(*To the* RINGMASTER) What part do you want me to be? I have
never been in this sort of Circus before, and I am not sure what
I can do. I play the piano a little bit, and I can dance a little,
but. . . .

RINGMASTER: Today, and today only, you will be allowed to see the
show, to sit up high on the seat reserved just for you, to look at
the show, to see for yourself what is going on. You may come and
take part, talk to any of our stars, and then, when the Circus performers have finished, you may make your choice of what part
you will play in our Circus of Life. Now, if you will take your
seat, the show will begin.

(The RINGMASTER *indicates her seat to LC, and the* CLOWN
accompanies ANNA LU *to it. During his movement the*
BALLADEER *once more sings, and the lights dim on the rest
of the set.)*

BALLADEER: Anna Lu who had been a mere snip of a girl just a
short time ago was finding herself on the brink of life, entering the
arena as a full-time performer. Just what part she would play was
still unknown to her, but she came into the venture with eyes wide
open with wonder and amazement. She knew there were lots of
performers in any show and it took all kinds to make the show
operate. She didn't dream of all the possibilities, nor did she know

all of the problems involved. But there she sat, perched on her own private bleacher, ready to see what the Circus of Life held for her.

(Sing Stanza 2)

Stanza 2

> Oh tell us do, Pretty Anna Lu,
> With your blue eyes all aglow,
> Is there a place just made for you
> In the exciting world of our show?

(The light dims out on the BALLADEER, *comes up slightly on* ANNA LU *and the* CLOWN *on the bleacher.)*

ANNA LU: Mr. Clown, I'll bet you were excited the day you joined the big Circus of Life, too. Do you remember it? Was it like this? Were you all covered with goose bumps, did you feel chills up your spine? Golly, I can hardly wait to be in the show—a real performer! *(mock concern)* But whatever can I do, what can I be? Mr. Clown, what do you think I can do? Where can I find out?

(The CLOWN *indicates the center ring where the* RING-MASTER *is standing, ready to introduce the first Act. Lights up.)*

RINGMASTER: Ladies and gentlemen, for the first attraction of the Circus of Life we present to you at this time one of the most outstanding performers of all time. This act is not a new one, but as old as time itself. The Circus of Life has never been without such performers as the one we are now to see. Miss Veri Prevalent, our bareback rider, in the standard favorite of all time, the Endless Circle of Routine.

(Music up, light on Bareback Rider who comes to a bicycle in the center of the ring and begins to ride it in a circle. The act goes on for a minute or so with ANNA LU *becoming a little concerned. The light comes up on her, music down, and she is heard speaking to the* CLOWN.)

ANNA LU: Is that all she does, go around and around in that circle? *(*CLOWN *nods)* Doesn't she ever get tired of it, doesn't she ever do anything else at all? Surely she must want to do other things. *(She jumps up)* Can I talk with her? Can I go down there and talk to her? *(The* CLOWN *nods and helps her down.)*

(To the BAREBACK RIDER*)* Excuse me. . . . Can you stop for a moment? Will they allow you to stop for a moment? *(The* BARE-BACK RIDER *stops)* I would like to talk to you for a minute, to ask you some questions.

BAREBACK: *(stopping)* Very good, I will try to answer your questions.

ANNA LU: I don't know how to ask you this exactly, but I was wondering . . . .

BAREBACK: Why I do this. Is that your question?

ANNA LU: Yes, that is what I want to know. Why do you do this?

BAREBACK: Your question is very easy to answer. I have always done this, I was taught to be a rider of the circle of routine very early. It began when I was a very small girl and watched my mother doing the same act. Every day she would begin her ride in the same way. She would first awaken all of the family, ask them to hurry and get ready for work or school. Then she would fix our breakfast, check our appearance, hurry us off to school, send my father off to work, and begin her own task of keeping the house.

ANNA LU: And you learned to do this from her?

BAREBACK: That is partly true. I also decided for myself that this was the best thing for me to do. I had seen others doing daring acts on the highwires and trapeze. Others could ascend to these heights, but I liked it closer to the ground, near where I was brought up, in the same manner in which I grew up. My act was a little different from my mother's, to be sure. I added a few features such as watching certain television programs during the day, or attending a bridge club each Tuesday night. I added an occasional trip someplace to give it a little more color, but on the whole I took the same type of act as my mother had. I like it.

ANNA LU: It keeps you busy all the time, I'll bet.

BAREBACK: All of the time. It seems that I hardly finish one routine until I am ready to start in on another. But this keeps me from worrying too much about the world problems, or community causes. I believe others can take care of them better. My place is in my routine where people in my family can depend upon me because they know where I am and what I am doing. *(She begins to ride again.)* Not everyone likes my act, they don't care to try it for themselves. But I am happy, and the Circus of Life can hardly do without me. You should consider it for yourself. *(She rides off.)*

ANNA LU: *(calling to her)* Thank you for answering my question. Maybe I will think about it. *(To the CLOWN)* But I don't understand where she is going other than around and around in the same circle. I would think it could get a little monotonous, like being in a rut. Doesn't she ever get dizzy from it, doesn't she ever lose her balance and feel that she is going to fall off? *(The CLOWN nods his head).* Do you think I should get into the act, Mr. Clown, really? I'm serious. I don't have a lot of talent, but I think I could make a good housewife, a good mother—a good dependable woman like this performer. Do you think I should? *(The CLOWN shrugs his shoulders and indicates that the RING-MASTER is about to speak again.)*

RINGMASTER: Ladies and gentlemen, it is our very happy honor to present our second major attraction of this show. High, high above the heads of us all we will find our next performer, walking the tightwire of success, our next attraction, Miss Dee Termined.

> *(Music is heard as she comes to the gilded ladder ready to climb to the top. ANNA LU and the CLOWN hurry back to the seats, and just as the performer is about to start up the ladder she looks at the BAREBACK RIDER who is still performing and shakes her head sadly. The BAREBACK RIDER stops abruptly and confronts the TIGHTROPE WALKER.)*

BAREBACK: I suppose you are shaking your head because you think your act is better than mine.

WALKER: I said nothing of the sort. I only shook my head. I hope that I am free to do that.

BAREBACK: And I am free to be whatever act I want to be in this Circus. If you do not like it, then you do not need to watch it.

WALKER: I only feel sorry that so many of you waste your time in that routine. The Circus needs more accomplished performers like me.

BAREBACK: And what accomplishment is there to walking a tightwire that is not also found in the work I do here on the ground? If the show were made up only of tightrope walkers, then it would collapse. My routine is the backbone of the show, and you are the exception to the rule, the "freak" of the show.

WALKER: *(angry)* How dare you call me a freak! I have never taken an insult like that from anyone. If I am a freak, then you are a misfit, and a nobody. Because I refuse to allow myself to be shackled to the ground, to fall into the rut of routine where I would shrivel and die, because I dare to rise above the mundane, you are jealous and call me freak. I am a free and independent performer; and you are a slave and a servant. I am a star and shine brightly in the constellation of performers while you are a mere firefly that glimmers occasionally in the dark but never shines for all the world to see. You are jealous.

BAREBACK: I am jealous, you say? I am ashamed of you. You deny everything that a woman is meant to be. You climb that ladder to achieve success at a price too dear for any woman to pay. You embarrass me and the others like me with your forward ways and your hardness. A woman is supposed to be kind, gentle, loving, and dependable. She is not supposed to be competition in business, away from the home most of the time, ruthless in her pursuit of success.

WALKER: I refuse to talk any longer to someone so naive and stupid as all that. *(She starts back up the ladder as* BAREBACK *exits.)*

ANNA LU: *(jumping down)* Wait a minute, wait a minute, please. *(She comes to the ladder, the* CLOWN *following)* Before you go up, I would like to talk with you.

WALKER: What about, my child?

ANNA LU: About your act and why you climb to such heights.

WALKER: I climb there because I believe that a woman has a right to be all that she can, to live as daring a life as any man. For centuries we have been treated with less rights, less respect as persons. We have stood back in the shadows while the show was carried on the backs of the men. We have handed them their properties, applauded their actions, and helped them go on when they fell. But we did not dare to climb to the top ourselves. We were afraid. And we were kept back.

ANNA LU: But you do not believe that this is true any longer? You believe that any woman can do as you are doing, that even I could do it?

WALKER: It takes a woman who is willing to pay the price of freedom, who is willing to be responsible, to compete, to take harsh blows that can come when you climb up that high.

ANNA LU: But isn't it frightening up there—and lonely?

WALKER: Frightening and lonely? I guess at times it is. But there is adventure there and with adventure there is always a little risk. It can be lonely at times, especially when others like the bareback rider can't understand what you are doing and can't communicate. But you find friends and get to know persons in ways you never achieve in that routine act below.

ANNA LU: I should think it would be very exciting climbing like this, but it must be very difficult and very tiring.

WALKER: It is hard at times. You have to be on the go constantly to be sure that you are at the right place at the right time with the right people. You can't sit by the way, or get in a rut and expect to achieve your goal.

ANNA LU: But can't that be something of a rut, too—climbing to the top day after day? The bareback rider goes in circles and you go up and down. I don't see the difference.

WALKER: Perhaps you are too young, or too inexperienced, my dear. Just remember this little jingle that I have always said to myself.

The ultimate aim of a woman, my dear,
Is to climb to the top in her chosen career!

ANNA LU: *(repeating)* The ultimate aim of a woman, my dear,
Is to climb to the top in her chosen career!

(The lights begin to shift from the ladies to the BALLADEER. During the darkness the two performers leave the stage and the PUPPETS take their place on the platform. Light on BALLADEER.)

Stanza 3

Oh tell us now, Pretty Anna Lu,
While watching our Circus of Life,
Do you find in our show any kind of clue
That gives meaning to all of your strife?

BALLADEER: *(Sings Stanza 3 once through.)* Our little lady was already seeing behind the scenes in the Circus of Life. It called for more than just a decision of what she wanted to be. It seemed to involve a matter of which is the right thing, the proper thing, and not just the best thing. But Anna Lu still had much more to see in the Circus of Life before she would be ready to make her decision about her own part.

(Lights out on BALLADEER and up on RINGMASTER, slightly on ANNA LU and the CLOWN on the bleachers.)

RINGMASTER: And now for a feature attraction that is surely a favorite of most people, and will warm your heart with a feeling of joy, we present for your entertainment and enlightenment the

famous Tragic Trio, the only human puppets in the world who
are willing to admit it. Ladies and gentlemen, the Tragic Trio.

> *(Lights up on the* PUPPETS *on the stage who sit loosely but
> begin to come to life as the strings above them move a
> little. This routine should be one of simple movements that
> demonstrate such things as eating, drinking, dressing, and
> other habits or tastes that are dictated by culture. After
> they have done their routine,* ANNA LU *comes to the plat-
> form to speak to them. The* CLOWN *accompanies her. She
> is entranced and delighted with them at first.)*

ANNA LU: *(to the* CLOWN*)* Oh I like them, I like them, I like them.
They are wonderful and funny *(suddenly dark)* but can they
speak? Oh, it would be terrible if they couldn't speak. *(The*
CLOWN *points to the* PUPPETS.*)*

PUPPETS: *(together with motions)* Do we speak? Do we speak?
　　　　　　　　　　Certainly we speak! What a silly
　　　　　　　　　　question from a girl!
　　　　　　　　　　Do we speak? Do we speak?
　　　　　　　　　　Certainly we speak! What a silly,
　　　　　　　　　　silly question from a girl!

PUPPET I: I can speak, I can speak very well.

PUPPET II: And I can speak, very well, too.

PUPPET III: Of course I speak, of course, I can speak, and I speak
very well, too.

ANNA LU: *(incredible but delighted)* You DO speak!

PUPPETS: Yes, we speak. *(To each other)* What a silly little girl.

ANNA LU: *(embarrassed)* I'm sorry, I guess that was a rude thing to
say. But I am happy to know you do speak because I want to
ask you some questions, too. You see, I am watching the Circus
to decide what I want to do in it soon. I was interested in your
act; it was very entertaining.

PUPPETS: You're going to join the circus? *(She nods.)* That's good!

PUPPET I: Providing, of course, you pay attention to advice from
above.

ANNA LU: *(looking up)* From above? Up there? In heaven?

PUPPET II: Oh, my goodness, not so high. Just *(points)* up there
behind the curtain, out of sight, behind the scenes.

PUPPET III: Just remember to do what you are told. It is easier if
you don't try to think for yourself—just do as you are told.

PUPPET I: Remember that 9 out of every 10 doctors smoke Fortune Cigarettes. People who know, who really count, smoke Fortune, drink Albert's ale, wear Ivy League Clothing.

PUPPET II: And remember that if you want to be healthy, wealthy, and wise you should join the Monday Ladies' Luncheon Forum, the Tuesday Woman's Coffee Club, the Wednesday Modern Women's Political Protest, and on Thursday . . . .

PUPPET III: On Thursday you purchase your new car, the latest of the models which takes only 36 months to pay; you plan a trip to Europe with 36 months to pay; and you get the latest refrigerator in decorator colors, you add a new stove that thinks for you, select a telephone in each color for each room so you are only a step away from the world when it rings . . .

ANNA LU: Golly, you three do talk. I can hardly keep up with you.

PUPPETS: Keep up with us! Think how hard it is for us to keep up with . . . .

PUPPET I: The Joneses.

PUPPET II: The Smiths.

PUPPET III: The Astors and the Vanderbilts.

PUPPET I: The Rockefellers and the Fords.

PUPPET II: The President and his wife, and the chairmen of our board.

PUPPET III: Or the egg-head elite, and the robust outdoor sports.

PUPPETS: You think you have it rough; look at us. (*They sag to the floor of the platform.*)

ANNA LU: (*distressed*) Wait, wait a minute. What has happened? (*To the* CLOWN) What is wrong with them? Are they dead? What is the matter? Where is all their pep, their spark?

(*The* CLOWN *indicates above*)

ANNA LU: Oh dear, they have to wait until somebody else pulls the strings to bring them to life? (CLOWN *nods*) I don't think that is good; I don't think I could like that.

PUPPETS: (*suddenly coming to life*) Wouldn't like it? Now, now, don't be a silly girl again.

PUPPET I: Let's take music for example. Do you want to have to study all your life to know what is good? Do you want to have to take a chance on some poor performance, bad record, costly mistakes?

PUPPETS: (*singing and dancing*)
Just listen to the Top Ten,
They'll tell you what is good!

> Just listen to the Top Ten,
> *They'll* tell you what is good!

PUPPET II:

> They'll put your name upon their list
> And tell you what to buy.

PUPPET III:

> They'll send you lots of records
> And you'll never wonder why!

PUPPETS:

> Because they choose it for you
> And tell you what is good!
> They help you make decisions
> In a way you NEVER COULD!

ANNA LU: But music isn't everything. There are lots of other things I would like to choose myself.

PUPPETS: You are getting impossible, little girl.

ANNA LU: I'm sorry.

PUPPET I: Better to be safe than sorry. Never trust an untried product; buy name brands; you can know you are safe and never sorry.

PUPPET II: Your life can be much simpler if you place it in their hands *(points upward)*. You don't need to worry about lots of things like politics, movies to see, magazines to read, courses to study, clothing to wear.

PUPPET III: Food to eat, homes to buy, cars to drive, and religion to practice.

ANNA LU: *(surprised)* Religion?

PUPPETS: Of course, religion. *(They do this routine.)*

> Bow your head, say your prayers,
> "It's time to pray."
> Pass the plate, pledge your tithe
> "It's time to give."
> Join a circle, lead a group,
> Hear a discussion, attend a meeting,
> Believe in God, sing a hymn,
> Stand up, kneel down,
> Turn around, be converted,
> Or be saved.
> BUT BE RELIGIOUS—do as we say.

ANNA LU: *(perplexed)* It seems to me there are some things that a person ought to decide for himself. Can't I make decisions for myself?

PUPPETS: Silly, silly, silly little girl. There is comfort in conformity and pain in other things. Why not join the team? You have fewer frustrations, less worry, more comforts, more things.

ANNA LU: *(walking away)* But what happens to Anna Lu if I do? What happens to me?

> *(The* PUPPETS *collapse on the platform lifeless.* ANNA LU *and the* CLOWN *start back toward the bleachers with* ANNA LU *a little confused and perplexed. The* CLOWN *tries to make her smile but with only partial success. As they are about to reach the bleachers, a gong sounds, the lights dim and the* RINGMASTER *appears.)*

RINGMASTER: Behold, ladies and gentlemen, the wonders of wonders about to appear before your eyes at this moment. From the distant lands, from the tropical jungles, from the modern metropolis, from every point of the earth comes an attraction that rivals all others in our Circus of Life. She is the queen that is honored in all history, she is the beauty that is worshiped in every place, she is the goddess who holds sway over the minds of men everywhere. Our next attraction: The Image of Feminine Charm!

> *(The music begins, the lights dim except for the* DIVA *who comes in held aloft by several males. They are attired as slaves, she is dressed to suggest sensuousness. They parade her around the stage, lower her and she begins a simple dance in which she is in complete charge of the scene, the males virtually crawling at her feet. The dance ends with all the men prostrate on the stage, the* DIVA *standing in a sensuous pose in the center of them. At this point the music stops and* ANNA LU *jumps to her feet.)*

ANNA LU: *(shouting)* Wow! *(coming to the* DIVA*)* Gee!

DIVA: Wow? Gee? What kind of language is that for a young lady to use?

ANNA LU: Well, I mean—Gee—I mean, what should I say?

DIVA: Certainly not "wow" and "gee." *(Claps hands and the men run off the stage.* ANNA LU *looks in amazement after them.)* Why are you staring? That isn't proper either!

ANNA LU: I was just looking at those men.

DIVA: Yes, I could see that you were. But it still is not polite to stare—not for a young lady.

ANNA LU: I'm sorry, but I was surprised.

DIVA: Don't show it that way. If you need to act surprised, that is fine, but don't show surprise unless it helps your cause.

ANNA LU: Helps my cause? I'm lost. I don't understand what is going on. I can't say "wow" or "gee" or stare, or act surprised. What am I supposed to do?

DIVA: Be yourself, my dear, be yourself. It's as simple as that.

ANNA LU: I suppose so—if you know who you are. I thought I knew, but now that I am here at the Circus I'm not so sure.

DIVA: A woman is first and last and always a female. Remember that and you can't go wrong.

ANNA LU: A woman is first and last and always a female?

DIVA: That is right. You can wear all sorts of clothing, change the style of your hair, work at many different jobs, speak a thousand languages, sing, dance, study—but no matter what you do you are a female. This is important to know.

ANNA LU: I guess it must be, but I'm a little confused. Can I ask why?

DIVA: You're still young and probably don't understand. So I will tell you why. *(looks at the* CLOWN.) Why don't you go sit on the bleacher again, Funny Face? *(The* CLOWN *looks at* ANNA LU *who finally nods approval.)*

ANNA LU: *(indicating the clown)* He's my friend, and he's nice.

DIVA: Then you do understand what I'm talking about already.

ANNA LU: I do?

DIVA: You are making the most of your femininity, your charm. You are playing the part you are meant to play; you are being yourself, a female.

ANNA LU: Well, how about that! Gee—I mean—well, I didn't know that.

DIVA: When you know it, you are much the stronger and the wiser, believe me. Those men you saw here with me know it, too.

ANNA LU: They certainly did act strangely. Did you have some kind of spell over them, maybe?

DIVA: Spell? Perhaps you could call it that. All I do is make the most of who I am and what I have to work with—my femininity.

I know that this attracts men, and I manage to get what I want, be what I want, do what I want by taking advantage of the situation—if you follow my thinking.

ANNA LU: I'm not so sure. I'm kinda young, you know.

DIVA: And you should learn it while you are young. The lipstick you chose, the perfume you wear, the way your dresses fit. The hair style you choose, the way you walk, the way you talk, the way you look. These are all part of what you do to be feminine. Remember a woman is a female first, last, and always.

ANNA LU: Oh, I won't forget it—but is this really the kind of part I should consider playing in the Circus of Life?

DIVA: Is it the kind of part you should consider? It is the part you are, my poor young thing. You don't choose to play it, you are it. You just make the most of it. Look at the movie stars the men flock to see—the ones you dream about being someday. Do they really have that much talent and ability—or do they use a little trick now and then to sell themselves as beautiful, desirable, and valuable, especially to men?

ANNA LU: I don't think I ever thought about it that way.

DIVA: Of course not, but you should begin. Now I'm not suggesting that all women can be famous movie stars or fashion models, but they can gain some of the good things of life by remembering what I have told you. Admiring glances from other women, and second looks from the men, popularity, success, achievement, fun, perhaps fortune can come to the woman who makes the most of her feminine charm. Get in the style shows, keep up with the fashions. Change your hair style, select a new shade of lipstick. Add some eye make-up, try a new perfume, and always keep the men interested in you as a feminine being. It's natural, it's good, and it's the way a woman can find her real happiness and strength. Do you understand what I am trying to tell you?

ANNA LU: (quietly and with wide-eyed innocence) What you are talking about is—sex? Is that it?

DIVA: (laughing) Oh, my poor little naive darling. Yes, that is what I'm talking about—sex. But for now you can think about being attractive, charming, and appealing. Later you may learn what a powerful thing you have to use with femininity. (She claps her hands and the men reappear. She indicates that she is ready to leave. They take her out as they brought her in.) Remember what I told you my sweet. A woman is first, last, and always a female —so make the most of it.

ANNA LU: I'll try to remember, I guess, but there are a lot of other things I wish I could have asked about. (*Turns to go back to the bleacher and the* CLOWN. *She nearly walks into the* RINGMASTER.) Oh, excuse me, I didn't see you standing there.

RINGMASTER: You certainly have a puzzled look on your face, Anna Lu. I hope you are enjoying the Circus. We have only one more act before the grand finale. Are you enjoying the show?

ANNA LU: I wish I knew. I thought I was—but now I'm not so sure. I thought it was going to be easy to decide what I wanted to be in the Circus of Life but now—

RINGMASTER: Suppose you hurry to your seat so we can have our last number. It will prove to be exciting for you, I know. (ANNA LU *does so*.) And now, ladies and gentlemen, we present the final act of our Circus for your entertainment and enlightenment. This act comes to us at great expense and much effort. Just how many and how much are involved we are not sure. But we are happy to present it to you, anyway. It is the great act of Training that occupies a central spot in our Circus of Life. It is our pleasure to present the greatest performer of them all in the Act of Training, Mrs. Modern Mother.

> (*Music starts up and the animals all flock on the stage with the* TRAINER *entering with them. She puts them through a little routine act which fascinates* ANNA LU *who applauds each stunt that the animals perform. At one point the* TRAINER *is unable to get an animal to do the trick. The* TRAINER *begins to wipe a tear from her eyes. The animal comes penitently to her side, receives a pat on the head, performs the trick, and the act goes on. At the conclusion of it* ANNA LU *comes to meet the* TRAINER *with the* CLOWN *at her side.* ANNA LU *stands applauding as the animals run off the stage.*)

ANNA LU: I like that, very, very much.

TRAINER: Thank you, young lady. It isn't easy work, but it is very rewarding and very important in this Circus, believe me.

ANNA LU: It must take a long time and a great deal of work to train all those wonderful animals so well.

TRAINER: It takes both a lot of time and a lot of work, and it also taxes one's imagination to find the best ways to do the trick.

ANNA LU: I'm sure it must require imagination.

TRAINER: Take that one trick just a moment ago that nearly failed. I had worked very hard to get that little rascal to learn his trick properly. I had tried everything I knew to make him do it. Finally, I had to resort to my imagination and use an old trick of my own. I acted hurt, and this did it.

ANNA LU: Why would that make him do his trick?

TRAINER: That is where the real value of this training comes in. You see, I have looked after these animals since they were born, given them lots of love and attention, and training, too. They are attached to me in very strong emotional ways. And when I act hurt or when I cry, I can usually bring them around to doing the tricks I taught them to do.

ANNA LU: It is sort of like a mother and her child.

TRAINER: I guess you can say that, but I suppose I make a little more of it than just that. Some people accuse me of exploiting my advantage at this point, building on my upper hand. The dependency that I have coming from my trainees can be used to good purposes as well as foul, I suppose.

ANNA LU: I guess it depends in part on what you do with this power, is that it? (TRAINER nods.) I don't know, but I would think this could be a very big act in the Circus.

TRAINER: Could be? My dear, it is probably the biggest act. And there are more women trainers than you can crack a whip at. In the nursery, in the home, in the school, in the Cub pack, in the church—everywhere the training is being done by women, by mothers, by persons like me who see the value and the need for this kind of training in the Circus of Life.

ANNA LU: Is it good that women do all of this training, that you are the only one or the major one to train your animals?

TRAINER: Some people argue against it, but I don't see them doing much about it. If they think men should be involved in the training, then they ought to get in it and stop talking about it. If they think that it is harming some of the animals, then they should correct the situation. Actually, honey, I think some of the men who complain are about as confused about it as the animals.

ANNA LU: I guess maybe you are right.

TRAINER: I know that I'm right. And I think you should give some serious thought to taking up this role in the Circus of Life, my dear. They can have all the social climbing, and charm they want but for me the real strength and role for a woman is in the training acts. When you snap the whip, they come running, and they know just what to do. (*She does so and the animals come dashing back on the stage.*) See what I mean?

ANNA LU: (*as the* TRAINER *runs off stage with the animals gleefully playing around her*) Thank you for telling me about your act. I guess. (*She stands bewildered for a minute. Then runs to the* CLOWN) Oh, Mr. Clown, what am I going to do? I came to the Circus so excited that I could hardly breathe and I was looking forward to being in the show real soon, but now I don't know what to do. Can't you help me? Can't you tell me what to do? (*She looks at him for a moment, he smiles a little, shakes his head.*) Then what can I do? (*She walks to the bleacher as the lights begin to dim and leaves* ANNA LU *all alone in the single light that picks her out of the darkness. She is unaware that the* CLOWN *is no longer with her.*) Golly, Mr. Clown, I didn't think, it would be this hard to decide. When you think about the Circus of Life, it looks so big and wonderful and exciting, that you don't realize what it means to take part in it. You don't realize how important the decision is that you have to make. You just rush into it and then wham! It hits you. (*pause*) You know what I think? I think I need something to help me make up my mind, something besides what I saw here. You know—some sort of measuring stick or scale to weigh my decision in. I need something to help me see that it is the right one. You know what I mean, don't you . . . Mr. Clown? (*Turns to see that he is gone.*) Mr. Clown, Mr. Clown, where are you? (*She looks about in the darkness.*) Gee whizz, everybody's gone . . . and I'm all alone. And now I have to make a decision. It's kinda scarey making decisions especially when you are all alone.

(*The light comes up slightly, first on the ringmaster who is standing center, then up to reveal all the others standing in anticipation about the stage ready to break out in their acts.*)

RINGMASTER: You are alone only in what you decide, Anna Lu. All of us in the Circus of Life are waiting to see what your decision will be and how you arrive at your decision. You may discover in this lonely decision making what meaning your role will have in the Circus. We are waiting to welcome you when you decide, even though the show goes on.

The characters begin their acts with enthusiasm as ANNA LU stands and looks at them all. The RINGMASTER continues to call out the acts, the music plays. The CLOWN comes to ANNA LU's side again, and tells her in pantomime that he is interested in her decision. He asks her by signs about each of the acts and she indicates she isn't sure. This is the process that is taking place as the lights dim out leaving only the BALLADEER and ANNA LU visible. She is walking off and looking back over her shoulder toward the stage; the BALLADEER sings Stanza 4 as the curtain closes.

Stanza 4

Oh tell us true, Pretty Ann Lu,
After seeing all of these choices,
Confusion clouds your eyes of blue;
Can you find your life in any of these choices?

The Ballad of Anna Lu

Words by
SUE WHEELER SMITH

Music by
EMMET SMITH

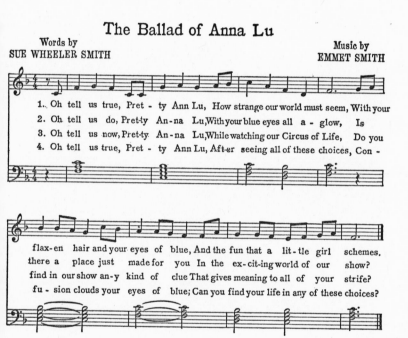

1. Oh tell us true, Pret - ty Ann Lu, How strange our world must seem, With your
2. Oh tell us do, Pret-ty An-na Lu, With your blue eyes all a - glow, Is
3. Oh tell us now, Pret-ty An-na Lu, While watching our Circus of Life, Do you
4. Oh tell us true, Pret - ty Ann Lu, Aft-er seeing all of these choices, Con -

flax-en hair and your eyes of blue, And the fun that a lit-tle girl schemes.
there a place just made for you In the ex-cit-ing world of our show?
find in our show an-y kind of clue That gives meaning to all of your strife?
fu - sion clouds your eyes of blue; Can you find your life in any of these choices?

PARABLE

Cast of Characters

QUEEN NANCY—a 20th century, animated, "modern" woman who finds herself a queen in the Middle Ages court which consists of her friends and acquaintances. She is open, naive, and without guile. She tends to be a little on the "loud" side and full of pep.

KATE—her friend of similar disposition, but a little less outgoing. She is quick to see through situations, explodes bubbles and delusion, and is intensely practical in an offhand sort of manner. She is ill at ease in the clothing of the court.

KING ALFRED—husband of Nancy, playing the kingly role to the hilt, being somewhat fun-loving in it all, but aware of what it means to be royal. He asks her permission to go out with the boys, to have a round of golf, etc.

PRINCE WILLIAM—son, teen-ager, tolerant of Mother.

PRINCESS CINDY—younger than PRINCE WILLIAM, mischievous, oblivious to the tag of "royalty," very natural.

COUNCIL OF MINISTERS:

MINISTER OF PUBLIC RELATIONS—keeping up with the Joneses

MINISTER OF THE INTERIOR—psychologist

MINISTER OF THE EXTERIOR—sociologist

MINISTER OF MORALS AND MORALE—religionist

MINISTER OF MISCELLANEOUS

SEVERAL ATTENDANTS AND PAGES

About this play:

Only royalty enjoyed in a day gone by the freedoms and luxuries now available to the modern American housewife and woman. At the disposal of royalty, and now for all American middle-class persons, were tremendous resources of such nature as to grant time and power to the privileged. History has held royalty accountable for what it did with what it was privileged to hold—in a word, stewardship. The question of who we are and with what we have to hold is the one with which this play deals. The device employed to carry the play is comedy or satire. The situation is one of imagination in which a woman of the average American home is discovered early one morning to be "royalty" in the Middle Ages. The honor and respect paid her by all, including her husband and children, serve to complicate her handling of her new privileged position. Her COUNCIL OF MINISTERS advise her at every turn, adding to the confusion of her life. A friend "KATE," helps retain balance in the midst of all the demands. The reign of our modern queen comes to an end, as it began, with the awakening from her dream.

The Setting

With the use of banners and simple furnishings the set is made to look like the court or throne room of a castle in the Middle Ages. Bright colors will accentuate the mood of the play in costumes as well as set. Most of the set can be brought into place by pages. The use of a scrim helps to suggest the idea of a dream at the beginning and end of the play. Behind it will be found a bed with a telephone stand and phone beside it. There is a throne on a dais on the stage and a few benches and chairs scattered about.

As the play begins the stage is bare with the attendants and pages quietly hurrying on the stage with parts of the set. As they work quickly and quietly, they are doing so to music and a little chant.

ATTENDANTS: *(as they work)* This is a play about royalty, royalty, royalty.

    This is a play about royalty of long, long ago
        (Repeat)

ATTENDANT 1: *(to the audience)* This story is a fairy tale, a fairy tale, a fairy tale.

    This story is a fairy tale . . . the subject of our show!

PAGE 1: *(to audience)* Which means, of course, that you can't believe one single word of it. *(The attendants take him in hand and glare at him. He hastens to add.)* Well . . . hardly any single word of it.

ATTENDANTS: *(continuing their work)* This is a play about royalty, royalty, royalty

    This is a play about royalty, of long, long ago.
    We are the lords and ladies, ladies, ladies,
    We are the lords and ladies who serve here in the court.

PAGE 2: But I'm different. I'm neither a lord, nor a lady. I'm a page! A page! I'm not sure out of what book, but a page, and what is more I'm an unpaid page! It wouldn't be so bad if I got paid to be a page but unpaid paging is unfair. *(Produces a sign that reads "This Court is Unfair to Unpaid Pages." All the attendants point at him and say, "Fie," hiss, and then continue into their routine.)*

ATTENDANTS: This is a story about our queen, about our queen, about our queen.

    This is a story about our queen and the business of her court.
    We want you to meet her family, her family, her family . . .
    We want you to meet her family, the center of her life!
        (bring KING ALFRED on the stage)
    This is good King Alfred, Alfred, Alfred.
    This is good King Alfred. . . .

ATTENDANT 2: Who likes to think he is the boss around here, but he takes orders like all the rest of us. *(Attendants turn, glare, and shout, "Fie!")*

ATTENDANTS: *(as PRINCE comes on stage)* And this is young Prince William, William, William . . .

    And this is young Prince William, the playboy of the court.

PAGE 2: This play takes place in the year 1356 B.C., before cars, which hampers the style of Prince William a little, but let it be said to his credit that he drives a really cool customized coach.

ATTENDANTS: And this is Princess Cindy, Cindy, Cindy . . .
    And this is Princess Cindy, the darling of the court.
    (CINDY *skates in waving to the audience and collides with people
    and furniture to bring about a terrific crash.*)
PAGE 3: (*Enters with trumpet which he plays sourly.*)
    Ladies and Lords, Lords and ladies of the court of her majesty
    Queen Nancy, now hear this. . . .
ATTENDANTS: Who? Queen Who? (*Adlib disbelief in the name.*)
PAGE 3: Queen Nancy, as I said. Her Majesty, the Queen—Nancy.
ATTENDANTS: Nancy? (*Continue in disbelief.*)
PAGE 3: And what's wrong with Nancy—if that's her name, I mean?
ATTENDANT 1: Well, Elizabeth, perhaps—but Nancy!
ATTENDANT 2: Or Victoria, or Mary—or even Gertrude—but Nancy!
PAGE 3: Hold it, hold it, stop right there. The lady says her name
    is Nancy, plain ole Nancy, and that's that.
ATTENDANT 3: Queen Nancy, nice Nancy! What a monarch!
ATTENDANT 4: Queen Nasty Nancy, roughest ruler ever to reign.
PAGE 3: (*blows horn again*) Lords and Ladies of the court—now
    hear this, her Majesty Queen Nancy is about to awake!
                    (*As the lights come up slowly behind the scrim.*)
PRINCE: How about that, cats, ole mom is about to roll out of the
    pad!
ATTENDANTS: And this is good Queen Nancy, Nancy, Nancy,
    And this is good Queen Nancy, the star of our fair show!
    (NANCY *is in bed, sleeping so that her backside is elevated
    toward the audience. She is covered with a sheet or blanket
    and stirs slightly when the telephone beside her bed rings.
    She responds slowly, groping for the phone from beneath
    the cover until she finally finds it. She mutters into it. The
    call has been made by* KATE *who is among the attendants
    on the stage from which place she has dialed the* QUEEN.)
KATE: Rise and Shine, your Majesty. Can't sleep all day, you know.
NANCY: Hmmm? (*mumbles*)
KATE: Good morning, Nancy, this is Kate. (*Pause*) You awake there
    gal? (*Mumbles from Nancy.*) Time to get up, Nancy dear! Open
    your peepers and face the world. (*Mumbles. Kate gets boister-
    ous*) Hey, roll out of the sack, Nancy ole girl, we haven't got all
    day, you know. Now pull yourself together and get with it. This
    is no way for a queen to start the day!

ATTENDANTS: And this is good queen Nancy, Nancy, Nancy,
>And this is good queen Nancy, the *star* of our show.

KATE: Say something to me, Nancy! Just anything.

NANCY: *(Gives an enormous yawn into the phone as she sits up in bed, wearing curlers, beauty cream, etc.)*

KATE: Thanks honey. At least I know you are still breathing. Now suppose you get up so we can get you dressed and some coffee poured down you. We have a big day ahead of us today.

NANCY: What day is this, anyway?

KATE: What's the matter, don't they provide the queen with a calendar anymore? Better check into that. Sounds like insubordination to me. *(to attendants)* Hey, one of you free-loaders, what day is this, anyway?

ATTENDANT 2: July 21, Friday.

KATE: *(into phone)* July 21, honey. Friday.

ATTENDANT 1: 1356.

KATE: The year 1356, if you're interested.

NANCY: *(sleepy)* Thank you, Kate, you're kind to an old. . . . 1356! Kate, you're a scream, an absolute scream!

KATE: Yeah! That's what all the girls in the bowling league say when I roll three gutter balls in succession. Well, Your Majesty, if you are sufficiently out of the sack for us to come in and get you dressed, we'll get this royal day in the life of our fair Queen started. *(Hangs up.)*
>(NANCY *stands up in bed and begins to exercise as the scrim is raised.* KATE *approaches the bed.* NANCY *has her back to the audience and attendants.)*

>KATE: Hey, Charles Atlas, take it easy.

NANCY: *(Turns to see the court standing before her)* What! *(She yells and dives under the cover as the court bows.)*

ATTENDANTS: *(Bowing)* Your Majesty!

KATE: Now let's be a big girl, Nancy ole kid, and come out from under the covers. This is no way for a queen to act in front of her court. *(To the attendants)* Maybe you guys had better scram. Her Majesty is a little gun shy this morning. *(Attendants leave.)*

KATE: *(Seeing that all are out)* O.K., Your Highness. You can come up now.

NANCY: *(Peeking out from under the covers at foot of bed)* Have they gone? Is it safe?

KATE: The place is as vacant as the brain cavity of some royalty I could mention, but won't.

NANCY: *(Agitated)* Kate, what's going on? Tell me, are we having some kind of convention? Has William brought some of his friends home for another rock 'n roll romp? Who are these people?

KATE: You must have had a rough night. I told you not to eat all that marinated herring before retiring. These are the members of your court just like yesterday morning and the morning before that and the morning before that and the. . . .

NANCY: Court! Oh, don't tell me. Does Alfred know I'm in trouble? Have you called him, Kate, to get me a good lawyer? *(Stands up in bed and shouts.)* I don't care what you have accused me of doing. I'm innocent!

KATE: I wonder if herring ever ferments? *(To Nancy)* Hey, climb down off your flag pole and get serious. We have a full schedule for Your Majesty, and this is no way for a queen to be carrying on.

NANCY: Queen? Full day? *(Beaming and wild with ecstasy)* Kate, don't tell me I've won! I'm Queen for a Day! Kate! Have I? Don't pinch me, I might wake up. Queen for a Day!

KATE: Well, yes, I guess you are. At least. I rather think, however, that your subjects had a little longer period of time in mind—maybe for life?

NANCY: You don't make sense, Kate. Now I don't want to hurt your feelings, or offend you, but you really don't make sense.

KATE: Well, how about that? You flip your lid and rave like mad royalty, and I'm the one that doesn't make sense. Now come on, honey, let's get you out of these pajamas and into your royal robes. Where on earth did you pick up an outfit like that? *(Indicates the pajamas.)* You would think they could afford something a little better for a queen.

NANCY: *(Half aware)* There's nothing wrong with my pajamas. I got them from Neimann-Marcus in Dallas. Now, Kate, I'm just a little confused, and without any coffee in me it's rough. But you just said again "queen" and "royal robes" and I want to. . . .

KATE: If its coffee that you need, it's coffee that you get. *(Claps hands, a PAGE appears instantly.)* Say, kid, bring Her Majesty a pot of hot coffee and pronto. *(to Nancy)* We'll get you waked up yet.

NANCY: *(who has been looking with suspicion at KATE but suddenly yells to the PAGE)* And the morning paper. *(to Kate)* I'm going to find out what is going on.

KATE: And I think you should. But you can get better information out of the kitchen crew than you can out of that daily sheet. Do you know that they misquoted you in three places yesterday when you made that major policy speech at the opening of the new drawbridge? Three places!

NANCY: Major policy speech! Drawbridge! Kate, *(getting intensely serious)* Kate, you have been my friend for years now—many years. We double-dated in high school, we were roommates in college, and we cried at each other's weddings; we still play bridge once a week. Now, Kate, you have to help me understand something here. Promise me, you will.

KATE: Take it easy, honey, your coffee is on its way.

NANCY: I'm not worried about coffee, Kate. I'm worried about me. *(Draws a deep breath.)* Am I queen, yes, that's it, am I a real queen or is this a joke of some kind you and Alfred have cooked up?

KATE: Now, Nancy, I'm a little offended by that. Alfred and I have never ganged up on you except for your birthday surprises. Maybe the strain is too much. What you need is a good vacation. Off to the seashore for a month. That's what you need.

NANCY: You haven't answered my question.

KATE: Since it somewhat silly, I thought I didn't need to. I guess this sudden return to reality is too much for a monarch every morning. Well, Nancy, let's do it slowly and simply. *(Coffee is brought in and set on the table. KATE begins to pour.)* What kind of house are you living in?

NANCY: What kind of house?

KATE: Just answer the question, drink a little of this coffee, and we will have you back in no time at all.

NANCY: Well, I live in a pretty nice house.

KATE: Pretty nice?

NANCY: All right, nice house! It is well built, sturdy, warm in the winter, cool in the summer. We have hot and cold running water and radio and T.V., each of us has a room for himself and . . .

KATE: And this is a queen's palace. What more could a woman want in life? You have a good family, a healthy batch of kids, all the conveniences known to mankind; you can sleep later than anybody for miles around because you have plenty of help.

NANCY: But it isn't any nicer than any other house on the street and I'm not any wealthier or more richly blessed than anyone else on this street.

KATE: I guess not—seeing as how yours is the only family on the street. On the whole lousy hill, if you don't mind my putting it that way.

NANCY: *(deliberately)* We have a whole lousy—I mean, we have a hill all to ourselves? Alfred, William, Cindy, and me?

KATE: And a few score servants, attendants, lords and ladies—the usual gang that hangs around royal households.

NANCY: I have servants?

KATE: Well, honey, I don't recall seeing you out beating the rugs, or stoking up the furnace or the cooking stoves, or butchering the beef, or milking the cows, or sewing up your dresses, or doing up your hair, or . . .

NANCY: I told Alfred that if he would get the sewing machine fixed I could do some of my own sewing, and he has promised me a hair-drier for my next birthday.

KATE: I guess royalty has a right to be a little eccentric at times. It makes history a little more interesting to read. But let's finish that coffee and get you dressed. Your Council of Ministers, that bunch of graft-seeking fakes, wants to meet with you.

NANCY: Council of Ministers? I am afraid maybe you are serious when you call me "Your Majesty."

KATE: Oh, I know I ought to be a little more respectful and address you always as the Queen, Your Highness, and Your Majesty, but I must admit it gets a little stuffy when we spend so much time together.

NANCY: Oh, don't misunderstand, Kate, I don't want you to change for the world. I was just wondering. *(Suddenly)* Hand me the morning paper, will you, please?

KATE: Sure, but why don't we get dressed first?

NANCY: I just want to check something, it won't take a moment. *(Scans the paper which is a scroll.)* Here, here it is. *(Shocked)* 1356!

KATE: *(not understanding)* Yeah. Time flies, doesn't it? Let's face it, honey, you're getting older all the time. What say we put those aging royal bones into a regal gown? *(Looks at the pajamas as the lights dim, the scrim falls.)* Neimann-Marcus . . . can you beat that?

ATTENDANTS: *(Coming quickly on the stage, moving across and off as they chant)*
> This is a play about royalty, royalty, royalty,
> This is a play about royalty, of long, long ago.

And this is Princess Cindy, Cindy, Cindy,
And this is Princess Cindy, the darling of our court.

(CINDY *and* ATTENDANT 4 *come on stage.* CINDY *is skating by hoisting her skirts and follows after the attendant, skating circles around her, etc.*)

CINDY: Matilda, what does my mother do all the time that she is so busy?

MATILDA (ATTENDANT 4): Always asking questions. Now what do you want to know?

CINDY: I want to know why my mother is so busy all the time that she can't find time to skate with me.

MATILDA: Who ever heard of a queen skating? That's about as silly as asking your father to customize the royal coach so Prince William would be able to enter it in the drags.

CINDY: What's so silly about skating? I happen to like it, and think it's fun. And I'll bet mother would like it, too, if she wasn't always going some place for meetings.

MATILDA: Your mother is a very busy and important person and she is expected to go to lots of places.

CINDY: Is that what mothers are for—to be somebody to go places? Is that it, Matilda?

MATILDA: Well, being a queen does require a lot of time. You have to go to parties and teas, to the theatre, to fashion shows, to community service clubs, to CWF meetings, to political rallies, to precinct meetings, to art lessons, to women's auxiliary meetings, to ribbon cuttings and christenings, to the beauty parlor and shopping, to the reducing salon, to the fund-raising dinner for the symphony, to the PTA, and to . . .

CINDY: Maybe if I make an appointment with her we could get her to go skating. What do you think, Matilda? Huh?

MATILDA: (*Pulling her off stage*): I think we had better get our clothes changed. We have a music lesson in 30 minutes, and after that you have a bluebird meeting, and tonight you are supposed to be at the church for an officers' meeting. (*Exits talking.*)

CINDY: Do you think I will grow up to be like my mother, Matilda? (*Exits.*)

ATTENDANTS: (*Coming across the stage in the opposite direction as before*)
This is a play about royalty, royalty, royalty.
This is a play about royalty, of long, long ago.

And this is young Prince William, William, William,
And this is young Prince William, the playboy of the court.

(Enter WILLIAM *and* ALFRED *who are talking.)*

WILLIAM: But, Pop, be reasonable. Weren't you ever a boy? Didn't
you ever have any fun in your life? I'll bet you didn't! I'll bet
you were always sitting around with your nose stuck in a book,
always reading and studying dry stuff like history and math and
archeology. I'll bet you never even looked at a girl until you saw
Mom, I'll bet you never did. (KING *starts to say something.)*
What kind of grades did you make in school anyway? All A's
or maybe A+'s? I'll bet you did because you never wanted to
have any fun, never wanted to enjoy life. And I don't think its
fair for you to make me suffer the same way. Just because you
never wanted to be one of the boys, never wanted to go out and
make your mark in the world is no reason why you have to keep
me in chains too. *(The king starts to speak.)* I'm not going to
throw my life away by growing old before my time. I'm still
young and I want to enjoy life. And I won't take it lying down,
either. All the other guys at school drive cool-looking coaches,
but what about me? Just the plain, straight, ordinary, run-of-the
mill model such as you drove when you were a boy; it's probably
the same coach—grey with age, creaking in the joints. Maybe
it doesn't make any difference to you, but I'm the one who has
to hold up my head at school. Do you think any of the girls will
go with a guy driving an old beat-up wreck like that? Mom will
tell you that she didn't even notice you the first time. She noticed
the guys driving the slick coaches. You ask her; she'll tell you.
(Getting chummy.) Look, Pop, you're a good guy and all that
and I am proud to be your son, but why don't you look at it
from my point of view for once. If you will just let me have the
family coach, I'll even pay you a little each month for it and
you can get a new one. You need a new one, the neighbors are
beginning to talk. And then I'll tell you what I'll do with it. I'll
lower the back about six inches, take off all the gilt, paint it over
with a good coat of primer, put some different headlights on it,
take off the fenders in the front and put on some nifty new ones
from some other make of coach. We could pinstripe it in a few
places. What do you think? *(King starts to speak.)* You like the
idea? Good, I knew you would. I'll go tell Mom about it. *(Starts
to leave.)* And think of all the embarrassment it will save you
and Mom with my customizing the family coach like this. Now

when I have a date cuddled up beside me for a drive, the neighbors won't think its you and Mom trying to act young again. *(Runs off stage.)*

KING: *(Looks after*WILLIAM *for a moment, then turns to the audience)* I'm the king. Anybody surprised by that? Well, you should be. You people got a minute? I should like to chat with you. Let me get a chair out here to sit on first. *(Claps hands, a page appears at the wings.)*

PAGE 1: Yeah?

KING: *(a little startled)* I would like a chair to sit on to talk with the audience.

PAGE 1: *(pointing to one)* What's wrong with that one over there?

KING: Nothing, that will do very well. *(Waits to have it brought.)*

PAGE 1: Good, then what did you bother me for? *(Exits.)*

KING: *(Shrugs shoulders and gets the stool to sit on.)* Now, as I was saying, I'm the king. Oh, yes, they still call me that, tolerate me, that is. I haven't decided just yet if this is an honorary title or not. But that doesn't really concern you, I know. What I thought you might help me think about is Nancy and all she has to do. She hasn't been a queen forever, and so some of this is new to her. She has lots of spare time now to spend on being queen that she used to have to spend on the house, the kids, on my meals—that sort of thing. But all of that has changed, and I'm not sure about what it is doing to Nancy—or all of us. Now she can get the house cleaned in a jiffy, using her new powers. She can toss a meal in the oven in nothing flat and we can enjoy luxury items never before available except to kings and queens. But then that's what we are, so I guess we ought to enjoy it. But the problem is this: here is Nancy with all this new freedom, this new power, this new time. How is she going to use it? I try to advise her sometimes, but I can't make her decisions for her. I know the demands that her position places on her, I know she has time to take on more obligations but I just wonder if she really knows who she is. Oh well, I'm the king, at least, I'm sure of that much.

PAGE 3: *(Blows sour trumpet.)* Hear ye, hear ye. The Council of Ministers is now in session. Make way for her Majesty the Queen. *(to king)* Hey, mister, will you get that chair and yourself out of the way? How about a little respect here, huh? *(trumpet)* Her Majesty, Queen Nancy. (KING *shrugs shoulders, moves chair as the music starts and queen comes in followed by her council.* KATE *is with her.)*

NANCY: *(Seeing* ALFRED *who is taking chair from the stage.)* Alfred! Wait a minute, Al *(catching up with him),* what on earth are you doing here?

KING: *(Bowing)* Your Majesty, it may come as something of a surprise to you, too, but I am the king and I live here.

NANCY: Oh, that's wonderful, having you caught in this crazy situation, too. Where are the kids. Are they here?

KING: Your enterprising son is out trying to trade the family coach for a newer sports model, and your ingenious daughter is badgering your appointment secretary for a date with her mother.

NANCY: Oh, the poor dear. I have been busy—too busy this morning. I will hurry with this silly meeting and then we can all go out to dinner and a show. *(Starts for the throne.)* Come, sit up here with me and let's get this thing over with.

KING: I believe I will go look after Prince William and the family coach. Something tells me that even that hassle will prove more worthy of my royal efforts than a meeting with your illustrious Council of Ministers. *(Starts to leave.)* Oh, yes, give my regards to Lady Lancaster and the girls of the Parents-Tutors Association. Reassure them that I understand full well that fathers are parents, too. *(Exits.)*

NANCY: *(Calling after him as he leaves)* Al, Al, Alfred! Oh, phooey! Now I'll have to make up some excuse for him again.

PAGE 3: Your Majesty, the Council is assembled.

NANCY: *(Moving DR.)* Kate, oh Kate! (KATE *comes to her.)* What am I supposed to do now?

KATE: *(a little surprised)* It must have been more than the pickled herring. Well, do what you always do, honey. Call the meeting to order and find out what the boys want. Then after they have raved for a while, turn them off and adjourn.

NANCY: That's all there is to it?

KATE: That's all there has been to it for the last five years, but then you aren't quite your usual self today, so I'll not venture too many guesses. Let's get with it before the boys get too worked up.

NANCY: *(Taking her place on the throne)* Ladies and gentlemen.

PAGE 3: *(Sour trumpet)* Her Majesty, the Queen!

NANCY: *(regaining composure)* I mean to say, Lords and Ladies, the Council meeting is now in session. *(There is an awkward pause.*) Well, what do you boys have on your minds? (*Disturbance*) I mean to say, what have you gentlemen to bring before us today?

COUNCIL: (*Adlib all at the same time.*) Your Majesty, it appears to me, *etc.*

NANCY: Wait a moment, please wait a moment. One at a time. Just one. (*Looking over the group.*) Suppose you speak first. (*Points to the* MINISTER OF PUBLIC RELATIONS) Ladies first, remember?

MINISTER OF PUBLIC RELATIONS: Thank you, Your Majesty. I know you will see the wisdom in your decision to call on me first when I share with you all of the problems and concerns that confront us in the realm of public relations. (*Claps her hands as two girls come in from the wings.*) Let me begin by showing you the first problem, Your Majesty. We have to decide which it will be this year—hems up, or hats down? That is as simply as I know how to put it.

NANCY: Hems up or hats down?

P.R.: Yes. We either raise the hemlines on the dresses for this next year, or we must lower the height of the hats worn by the ladies in the land. But a decision must be made so that work can begin at once on a campaign all across the land to bring clothing up to date.

NANCY: (*Pause.*) Why?

P.R.: Why? Well, to keep the ladies garment guild in full production, of course, and to give the press something to write about. Your majesty cannot afford to pass up this opportunity to be photographed in the latest fashions at the Opera next fall. So we must decide hems up or hats down.

NANCY: If we want hems up, then Alfred would have to buy me the sewing machine to save money on a new wardrobe.

P.R.: Precisely, and this would start a trend all across the land which would greatly improve the sewing machine business. Your Majesty could please a lot of the business interests in this way.

KATE: What are you going to do about the hats, Your Majesty? If you go up with hems, do you have to come down with hats—to balance things out, I mean, and to avoid inflation?

NANCY: Inflation? What has this to do with inflation? I thought we were talking about fashions.

P.R.: Your Majesty cannot make a decision any longer without causing some change in the land. You either help inflate the economy or deflate the ego.

MINISTER OF THE INTERIOR: Did I hear the word "Ego"? Ego? Did I hear it?

KATE: The word was used, and the chances are 10 to 1 you heard it. You hear it before Freud is even born, good ear.

INTERIOR: I have been following this discussion most carefully, and I feel that there are psychological implications involved that need to be given much thought before springing into actions that would drive the country to the verge of mental or emotional collapse.

EXTERIOR: Or social deterioration, blighted slum conditions, and unemployment problems. Dissocial and antisocial groups will locate in suburban settlements and bring about islands of social unrest.

NANCY: What are you gentlemen talking about?

KATE: In brief, things could be in a real mess!

NANCY: Because of hems and hats?

COUNCIL: (in unison) Because of hems and hats.

INTERIOR: Does it ever occur to you what psychic states might be brought on in this land of ours if you raised the hems and lowered the hats. The men in this country alone, at the mere thought of raising the hem of women's dresses, well, they would absolutely panic—push the panic button.

MORALS: And *you* would have Freud rear his ugly head even here in the presence of these ladies! Fie!

INTERIOR: Freud has nothing to do with it. I was thinking of the anxiety created in the men when they have to pay for a new wardrobe, at a time when money is scarce and prices high. The shock of that news should prove good for a 5% rise in cases of neurotic anxiety.

P.R.: Which should be good for a 35% increase in the sale of tranquilizers. Your Majesty, this is too good to be true. The economy of the country can be altered by one simple choice you make about hems.

EXTERIOR: And hats! You people stay so close to the castle here that you don't know what is going on in the world all about you. But as Minister of the Exterior, let me assure you that things and people are not standing still.

KATE: People yes, things no!

EXTERIOR: What did you say?

KATE: People yes, things no!

ATTENDANT 2: Cuba Yes, Castro No!

COUNCIL: *(After a moment of stares)* 1356, remember! B.C.—before Castro.

KATE: This is ridiculous! We were talking about hats. Remember, gentlemen?

EXTERIOR: Exactly, and I was saying that the hat industry is every bit as much in need of a revival as the dressmakers.

MORALS: Did I hear someone say "revival"?

EXTERIOR: I said, "Revival." Of the hat industry, out in the small towns and villages, out in the countryside, the little businessman.

MORALS: We could use a good revival in this country—a revival of our sagging spiritual posture. We are becoming a nation of middle-aged people wearing spare tires. Flab everywhere you turn! We need to prop up the sag, we need to tone up the spiritual muscles of the people. We need a good revival—it would do us all good.

P.R.: And it will be good for the queen to be leading her people in this. She can be seen going to the revival with her family. Princess Cindy could walk in holding her father's hand, and young Prince William can be escorting the queen.

KATE: It would be more like it to say the queen would be dragging young Prince William by the hand.

MORALS: Let us not make light of things serious and sacred. Remember the words from the scriptures: Families that revive together, stay alive together!

KATE: That's from the scriptures?

MORALS: If not, it ought to be. Perhaps Her Majesty could use that catchy little, mouth-filling, inspirational phrase in one of her public speeches soon.

NANCY: I'm not sure I understand what it means, exactly.

INTERIOR: All of us are given to using thoughts of which we are only partially aware, consciously, that is.

EXTERIOR: Whole groups of people are driven by motivations of which they are completely unaware. They are led to doing things without knowing why. It's all in the subconscience.

INTERIOR: Subconscious! If you sociologist are going to use terms belonging to the psychologists, it would be well to learn them first.

EXTERIOR: It would seem to me that you psychologists could use all the support you can get. I wouldn't be too quick to judge. Anyway, how do you know I wasn't coining a new word to describe some newly observed phenomena?

INTERIOR: I have noticed a tendency on the part of your crowd to dismiss perfectly good words already in our language.

EXTERIOR: We expect soon to publish our own dictionary. Last week we coined 143 new words, and reclaimed 57 old ones with a new twist.

INTERIOR: There is something just a little subversive in this, Your Majesty, that perhaps ought to be investigated before it becomes a menace to our people. If our language is not good enough for our citizens, then our forefathers would have done something about it. Anyone who tampers with our language is tampering with our basic God-given rights as psycho-social organisms.

MORALS: Did I hear someone mention God?

KATE: I am sure that if anyone heard his name mentioned, you did. But I would suggest that you gentlemen not confuse the issue by introducing any authority higher than your own.

MORALS: Well, of course. But I do think we could add the phrase to our slogan, "Thus saith the Lord." It would give it more of a ring of authority. If we said, " 'The family that revives together stays alive together.' Thus saith the Lord," it would be a much more powerful motto for our people.

KATE: It sounds a bit ambiguous to me.

EXTERIOR: Wonderful word, wonderful word! I must add that one to my new dictionary. But tell me, don't you think we could show Her Majesty wearing a lowered hat as she makes this decree, and as she goes to the revival? This would establish a precedent for all the ladies of the land who would do as she does, and the hat industry would be helped, too.

INTERIOR: Excellent, excellent. Subliminal advertizing. Thousands will pass the hat racks and reach out automatically to buy a low model and will never be quite sure why. Wonderful!

P.R.: But only if the hems are raised. It has to be a top-to-bottom overhaul.

INTERIOR: Stem to stern.

EXTERIOR: Hems up, hats down.

KATE: Bottoms up! Tops down!

MORALS: Alpha and omega!

P.R.: How about posing Her Majesty for a few publicity pictures to launch the campaign to raise the economy of our country by raising the hem, lowering the hats. *(Claps hands for a photographer.)*

MORALS: And let it be printed in red-letter editions all across the land: Hems Up! Hats down! Her Majesty Queen Nancy decrees: "The families that revive together stay alive together! Thus saith the Lord!"

> *(The photographer enters, the* MINISTERS *begin to busy themselves with posing* QUEEN NANCY *in various ways with hem and hat being important, smiling, and with book or Bible, etc. During this routine the* ATTENDANTS *do a little dance as they chant.)*

ATTENDANTS:

> This is a play about royalty, royalty, royalty,
> This is a play about royalty, of long, long ago.
>
> And this is good Queen Nancy, Nancy, Nancy,
> And this is good Queen Nancy, the star of our show.
>
> But alas for poor Queen Nancy, Nancy, Nancy,
> Alas for poor Queen Nancy, she's getting lost of advice.
>
> And such is the life of royalty, royalty, royalty,
> And such is the life of royalty, it isn't always nice.

> *(*PRINCE WILLIAM *and* PRINCESS CINDY *come on stage with a roar.)*

WILLIAM: Mother! MOTHER! Get this monster off my back or I'm going to wrap a roller skate around her neck.

CINDY: Mother! MOTHER! William has been saying ugly things to me and pushing me around and threatening me.

NANCY: Now children, children. Let's remain calm. Settle down and keep very still for a moment until you can tell me what is the matter.

INTERIOR: You don't want to inhibit your children too much, Your Majesty, or it will lead to severe consequences later. Childhood trauma, you know. Very serious.

EXTERIOR: Repressed childhood hostilities can lead to gang formation and delinquency, Your Majesty. One must be very cautious in handling such psycho-social predicaments as this.

MORALS: And the gilt feelings that can result when a child is severely reprimanded must be handled with proper spiritual insight lest it warp his own cosmological and metaphysical perspective to life.

KATE: Can it! You guys are strictly for the birds, so why don't you take it on the wing and fly out of Her Majesty's hair for a few moments while she talks with her children. Scat! (*The* MINISTERS *leave as do the* ATTENDANTS.) O.K., kids, what's your beef? And it had better be good because your mother is one busy woman.

CINDY: But she is my mother!

KATE: I should hope so. No one else would claim either of you.

WILLIAM: Mother! Dad said I could take the family carriage and do a little work on it—streamline it a little, if you know what I mean—and so I was busy taking off the gilt and the crest when this devil on wheels comes skating right through the middle of it all, even climbs up on the upholstery with her skates. Now you make her stop it and keep her out of my way.

CINDY: Do you want to put me in chains, or how about a dungeon where the rats could eat me up, little by little.

NANCY: Cindy! Now, is that any way to talk? Where on earth did you get such ideas as that anyway?

CINDY: Afternoon kiddies show at the puppet theater in the courtyard. Boy, you ought to see it, Mom. Every afternoon at least ten puppets get murdered—real juicy like.

KATE: Maybe you do have a devil on wheels.

NANCY: Cindy, have you been bothering your brother?

CINDY: Can I help it if my silly brother puts his ole carriage in the path of my roller skates?

WILLIAM: There are acres of skating places she can use without having to get within a mile of me.

CINDY: A mile is too close, thank you. Why don't you all just ship me off to a camp somewhere so I can be out of your hair?

KATE: I'll start taking a collection for the fare right now.

NANCY: Now, Cindy, you know we don't want to ship you off anywhere. We only want you to be a good little princess so we can be proud of you. You know Mother is very, very busy and your daddy has more to do than he can get done being the king and so we need you to work with us. Why don't you skate on the other side of the castle and let William have this side where he is working?

WILLIAM: And stay on that side of the castle.

NANCY: I don't believe that Cindy is the only one to blame in this situation. You do have a tendency, William, to take over any place you land. Suppose you keep your mess confined to the royal garage and don't let the stuff lie in other people's way. You know you have an obligation to this family, too. I'm not always sure you remember what it is.

WILLIAM: Remember what what is—the family or the obligation?

KATE: If we ever need a nasty tongue to defeat the enemy, I have a nomination.

NANCY: William, that was not very kind. We do the best we can, but you know as well as I that there are many demands placed upon each one of us. I don't recall seeing you around the home much these past few weeks.

WILLIAM: That girl across the moat keeps me busy. Surely you can understand that. Don't tell me you have forgotten what it was like.

NANCY: No, I haven't forgotten. But suppose we all make up now and see if we can't be a little friendlier and happier together? O.K.?

CINDY: If he'll stay on his side of the castle.

WILLIAM: And if she'll keep out of my hair.

KATE: Now we understand how iron curtains get built. Well, you kids stand back, Mother is not quite finished with the day's duties and I believe that I see the long nose of a Minister of Miscellaneous poking its way into the court.

> (PAGE *blows a sour note again.*)

PAGE 3: Your Majesty, the Minister of Miscellaneous would like a word with you.

NANCY: I wonder what he wants.

KATE: Send him in, Boy.

> (MINISTER *enters with the attendants behind him and the rest of the* COUNCIL *trailing and still discussing things.*)

MISCELLANEOUS: Your Majesty, I beg your pardon for intruding so abruptly into the life of your lovely family, but there are a number of matters that require the urgent attention of Your Royal Highness and Her Council. May I begin?

KATE: I'm not worried about his beginning; I'm more concerned about his stopping. Miscellaneous has a way of accumulating things.

NANCY: Yes, please begin. Will all of you worthy ministers come hear the matter with me? *(They gather.)*

MISCELLANEOUS:
> The state of the world is in very bad shape
> And I believe that you all should know it!

ATTENDANTS: Know it!

MISCELLANEOUS:
> There are riots and revolts, delinquents and gangs!
> The restlessness surely does show it!

ATTENDANTS: Show it!

MISCELLANEOUS:
> There are people who clamor for glamor and sex!

ATTENDANTS: He said it!

MISCELLANEOUS:
> And those who wage war for propriety!
> There are people who drink, and those who say "NO!"
> There is turmoil in the whole of society!

ATTENDANTS: Society!

KATE: So what's your point?

MISCELLANEOUS: Oh, don't do that! Don't do that! I'm just getting warmed up.

KATE: And so is the temperature in this room. Can't you maybe cut it a little? We will never know the difference.

ATTENDANTS: Difference!

MISCELLANEOUS: Very well, I will come right to the point. I have requests from 314 different organizations that want support and the worthy name of our Queen to put on their lists.

> There is a fund for feeding the hungry hundred
> And a fund to help lose weight.
> There's a fund for saving stinkweed
> For the glory of the state.
>
> There's a club for wandering minstrels
> And a home for troubadours.
> There's a group of nature lovers
> Who want to move outdoors.
>
> There's a club for girls, incorporated,
> For ladies who are forty-one.
> There's a Mom-and-Dad club of archery
> Called the "William Tell Sons."

> There's a jumbo drive for peanuts
> To keep the elephants fed.
> There's a group of teen-age boys
> Who vote for lunch in bed.

KATE: Sound the trumpet; beat the drum; turn him off, somebody.

MISCELLANEOUS: Your Majesty, I have only 303 more items to list— quickly, of course.

NANCY: Perhaps you could submit the list in writing and we could consider it independently of this meeting.

MISCELLANEOUS: But they are of urgent needs, requiring immediate action.

KATE: And money!

MISCELLANEOUS: And we cannot afford to let these causes die.

KATE: Even if we can't afford it, period.

MORALS: I have a brilliant idea, Your Majesty. Let us add it to our campaign to lift the level of our country to an all-time high. We can call upon people not only to "Hems up! Hats Down! Her Majesty Queen Nancy Decrees: The Families that Revive To- gether Stay Alive Together! Thus Saith the Lord," but we can call upon them to make great personal sacrifices in order that the causes of mankind can be met around the world. The hun- gry can be fed, the elephants saved, and the troubadours given a home. Everyone sacrificing, giving of themselves without stint.

NANCY: And how do you propose that we accomplish such a feat?

MORALS: Simple. Have a cake sale, throw a benefit dance, sell candy. Everyone sacrificing.

> *(At this point every one of the* MINISTERS *begins to clamor for the* QUEEN's *attention with "Yes, Your Majesty, and what is more, etc.")*

NANCY: *(After a few moments of the clamor)* Alfred! Alfred! *(Runs from the group frantically looking for Alfred.)* Alfred! Help!

KING: *(Ambling on the stage)* Yes, my dear, you called?

NANCY: *(Rushing to him)* Alfred, I've found you. You will have to save me from these people. They are about to tear me apart; they are trying to drive me crazy. Help me, Alfred.

KING: *(Looking over the situation)* Hmmm! I see. Well, I shall see what I can do.

> *(Walks to the throne where he indicates that the trumpet is to be blown. The trumpet blows sourly.)*

PAGE 3: Your attention please, his majesty the King, King . . .

KING: Alfred!

PAGE 3: Oh, yes, His Majesty King Alfred wishes to speak.

KING: *(calmly)* My good people and dear subjects, I wish to dismiss this meeting but first I have a message from Your Queen. *(Bronx cheer.)*

> *(The people leave the stage with the exception of* KATE, *the* KING, *and* NANCY.)

KING: *(to Nancy)* And now, Your Majesty, I believe that a word is in order and then a nap. Allow me to say a few things before you rest. *(Claps his hands.)*

PAGE 3: Yeah!

KING: A chair for His Highness, if you please.

PAGE 3: How about that one, over. . . .

KING: Thank you. I'll save you the trouble. *(Gets the stool and returns to talk with* NANCY *who is flaked out in a chair with* KATE *fanning her.)* Now then, Your Majesty, there are a few things that one must consider if one is to be a queen—today or any day. First, royalty and luxury and power always involve responsibility. Responsibility always demands decision.

Decisions must be made by using some criteria of judgment.

Any judgment is based upon faith in certain principles and truths. And any faith is a personal responsibility that you alone must assume.

Kate can help, I can help, Even your Council of Ministers can help. But what you will do with who you are and what you have —this is an act of faith which you alone must decide.

Kate, Her Majesty needs to rest. And I have promised the Duke a round of golf on the royal green, so, if you would, please. *(Goes to* NANCY *and gives her a peck on the forehead.)* Sleep well, Your Highness. You will need your rest; your daughter wants you to go skating at 4 o'clock.

NANCY: Thank you, Alfred. You are, as always, a dear. *(To Kate)* Kate, I just knew things were all messed up when I awoke this morning. 1356! That just can't be right. It ought to be 1961.

KATE: *(Helping* NANCY *up and off the stage.)* What difference does it make? A queen is a queen in any age. Come on, off to bed with you.

(They walk slowly off the stage as the lights begin to dim on stage, with the light behind the scrim coming up. Someone else has put on the costume of the QUEEN—the pajamas—and is in the bed in the same position as at the beginning of the play. The telephone rings and we hear the voice of KATE. The voice of the QUEEN is heard from behind the bed.)

NANCY: *(Mumbles into the phone)* Hullo.

KATE: *(Brightly)* Good morning, Nancy ole gal, time to rise and shine. You can't sleep all day; you're not a queen, you know.

NANCY: *(Bolting upright)* What! What was that about a queen?

KATE: I said you can't sleep all day; you're not a queen, you know. They all died out with the Middle Ages—well, nearly all.

NANCY: What's the date?

KATE: July 21, 1961. I'm on my way over for coffee, so get with it.

NANCY: *(After a moment jumps up in the bed and energetically begins the exercises as the curtain closes.)*

CONSTRUCTION

Cast of Characters:

ART—a rather rough individual, capable of temper outbursts, unrefined, bothered by fears which are less obvious in his behavior and brave front. Served as a police officer before coming to this place.

SCHMIDT—an organizer who feels the need to whip things into shape, to structure the group with himself in a role of control and leadership. He is earnest, well-meaning, but a little self-centered in his efforts.

LYDIA—a fanatic in the religious sense who has little patience with those who differ with her. She is more of a moralist than a Christian and demonstrates insecurity in her dealings with foreigners. She is prejudice ridden.

ELIZABETH—a woman of high social standing and background. She is of a good spirit and well meaning but lacks insight. She thinks in terms unlike most of the others, but seeks to work with them. She is mindful of her station, however.

TERRY—a teen-age lad of about 17 or 18 years of age who is frustrated in not knowing where he fits into things, and he has not yet accepted a socially responsible role. He conflicts strongly with ART who represents for him authority, and also with LYDIA who represents unreasonable Puritanism. He is linked romantically to BETSY, the teen-age girl.

BETSY—a teen-age girl who is a little bewildered by all that whirls about her. She is eager to do well in life, and to make a good wife and mother someday. She is upset with TERRY's impetuousness, and given to tears at times of stress. She is relatively mature, however, and wholesome as a personality.

65

DOLLY—a woman of questionable character among this group. She is flirtatious in some instances, materialistic in others, and sensitive in some ways to the needs of others. She manages to avert difficulty within the group, as well as become the object of real scorn from LYDIA. She is earthy.

JOE—an exchange student who lives temporarily with this group of people. He is quiet, philosophical, and humanitarian. He is accepted in various ways by some of the group, rejected by others.

HANK—a minority group member, he is tolerated but relegated to an inferior status in the group. He is resentful at times, discouraged at times, shrewd on occasion. He and JOE understand each other's plight somewhat.

THE BUILDER—a human with human characteristics, though his role in the play is that of the Christ figure. He is strong, positive, direct, and wholesome.

About this play

It is symbolic and slightly otherworldly in that it is not located in any particular time or place and the characters are real only to the degree that they have characteristics of normal everyday personalities. In the misty flats of this never-never-land 9 persons find themselves together. All about them are materials and tools with which they are to do something. They are perplexed, fearful, and argumentative as they wait. Each one in turn finds fault with the others' ideas of what is supposed to be done with the materials at hand. Fear seizes the group when they become aware of others near by—unknown and unseen. As they are about to construct a wall to defend themselves from all outside forces, the BUILDER appears on the scene. This individual comes with a blueprint which was intended to be used in the first place. The materials are meant to be a bridge which will connect these persons with the others in a real sense. But fear, apprehensive and pride defeat the BUILDER who at the moment when hate erupts, speaks of human love and divine intention, and he is crucified once more. A few realize what they have done as the curtain falls.

Organ Prelude

Music that is mysterious and ominous in sound.

During the prelude the curtain opens, the lights begin to paint the set. Characters are seen in position, waiting and watching. They hold various positions, some pacing as the tenseness of the music builds. When the prelude is at its peak the action begins with Art throwing a tool to the floor with an oath.

The Setting

A stage that is rather barren appears with crates, lumber, bags of cement, stones, and tools piled all about. There is little illumination except of the direct acting area, with an illusion of distance or space all around. Isolation is the visual image achieved in the setting. During the second scene there is some evidence of a scaffold being used to construct a wall. To one side on the floor and unseen by the audience is the cross on which the BUILDER is crucified at the end of the play. At the beginning of the play there are fumes or smoke moving about, lights that catch only one or two performers at a time until they are up full by the end of the prelude.

ART: *(Throwing down the tool)* I've had enough! I'm getting out of this place. This is getting on my nerves. *(As he begins to leave.)* What the hell are we doing here anyway?

SCHMIDT: Sit down. You're not going any place, at least not now. *(ART pauses.)* Sit down. You're not in any hurry here.

ART: *(Challenging)* What was that crack, wise guy?

LYDIA: *(Authoritatively)* He told you to sit down because you aren't going any place. You have to wait like the rest of us, so sit down, he said.

ART: Butt out lady, butt out. This has nothing to do with you, and nobody was asking for your two cents worth.

LYDIA: *(Offended)* Well, I have never! What a horrible example of manhood!

ELIZABETH: Disgraceful behavior. I think someone should take this man in hand.

SCHMIDT: *(Coming to Art)* O.K., O.K., that's far enough I think for all of us. We had better cool down a little.

ART: *(Suddenly aware of the situation.)* Sorry, ladies, sorry. I'm just not used to this place, it has me jumpy. I'm usually not like this, but this gets on my nerves.

LYDIA: I know what you mean, so I accept your apologies. It is hard to sit here in one place and wonder and worry—never sure just what is going to happen.

ART: Can't we find something to pass the time; do something?

LYDIA: But what?

BETSY: *(From one side where she has been sitting with Terry)* I would like to know who is here. I always feel more comfortable when I know everyone else.

ART: I guess it wouldn't hurt to know each other's names—sort of silly considering how long we have been here without anybody asking names and stuff.

BETSY: In my youth group at home we used to do this at the beginning of each year—tell names—but we asked everyone to tell something more about himself so we could get to know each other better.

DOLLY: *(Swinging her foot)* Maybe you don't care about people digging into your past, Sweetheart, but as far as I'm concerned, it's nobody's business but my own.

BETSY: I only meant we could tell a little something about ourselves to help the conversation along. We don't have to do it at all if you don't want.

ART: I'm game. How about the rest of you? (*to* SCHMIDT) O.K. by you?

SCHMIDT: Fine by me. Suppose we let the little lady over there start us off since she knows the game.

BETSY: Well, I'm a teen-ager by the name of Betsy—one of those terrible persons you read about. I like lots of things, even school. I like to dance and go to movies, and to swim. I play the piano a little, and well, I guess that's about all. (*Looks at* TERRY.)

TERRY: My turn? (*uneasy to some degree*) My name is Terry. I like the same things as Betsy—except school, I guess. I'm nearly 18 and will have to register for the draft soon. That's all. (*Looks at* DOLLY)

DOLLY: Name: Dolly! I like to live, enjoy life. I don't think I need to reveal anything more.

SCHMIDT: C. A. Schmidt is my name; go mostly by "Schmidt." I'm a contractor by trade, make a pretty fair living that way, too. I'm a member of the Brothers of the Knighthood Lodge, a veteran of the First one, and I have three kids, all grown now.

ART: My name is Art. I'm a police officer back home. I'm also a member of . . .

TERRY: (*with a hoot*) Police officer! What do you know about that? Hey, Betsy, what are pennies made of? (*Laughs.*)

ART: What's so funny about being a cop, kid? Somebody's got to do the job and protect citizens from cut-ups and scatter-brain kids. Look, I don't want any trouble, but keep that up and it might come.

TERRY: Listen to the tough guy talk. Copper! (ART *starts to move toward him but* DOLLY *stops him by extending her leg.*)

DOLLY: We were having introductions, remember?

ART: Yeah, that's right. (*Returns to his place with anger still rumbling.*)

LYDIA: Are you finished? (ART *nods.*) Well, my name is Lydia Langston. I'm the mother of three children, two of them teen-agers like Betsy here. However, they don't do any dancing. We are Christians. We believe that people have to defend their homes and children from worldliness like that. "As a man is in his heart, so is he." Our family has much pleasure together anyway. I remember once when we were all on a trip—*(catching herself)* Oh dear, I'm not supposed to take so much time. I'll be quiet.

ELIZABETH: My name is Elizabeth Crimrod Beacon. My husband is the president of Beacon Industries. I'm dreadfully sorry that we have this long wait here, but I suppose we are doing the best we can. *(A pause while others wait.)* Oh, excuse me; I have nothing more to say.

ART: *(Indicating* JOE *and* HANK*)* O.K., fellows, your turn.

JOE: *(Looking first to* HANK *to get his cue.)* My name is Joe, well, not really, but my real name is so complicated that I have taken up the name Joe. I came from the Orient to this country to study dentistry. I have been here for several years, but plan to return to my country within two more years. I have a wife and two children.

HANK: My name is Hank, I am a student studying music. I want to be an entertainer someday. I'm not married.

ART: Well, now that is over, what can we do?

TERRY: Don't tell me the long arm of the law is stumped for something to do. Why don't you go chase teen-agers and hand out tickets or maybe help old ladies across the street?

SCHMIDT: I think you had better keep quiet, young man. We don't need any fights yet.

TERRY: It might liven things up a little. *(Starts to stand)* I'm getting bored and the cops are always good for a little fun.

BETSY: Terry, I think you have said enough—too, too much. You just can't learn to keep your mouth shut. *(Starts to cry.)*

TERRY: Good Lord, all I said was—well, why do you have to start crying at that? You know how I feel about cops.

ELIZABETH: Please, let's not get into a quarrel. We would all regret it and I believe we can find something better to do with our time here than to think evil thoughts about each other.

SCHMIDT: Maybe I'm wrong, because I'm just a plain ole contractor, but what I think we need is a little organization, some system to help us get things done.

LYDIA: You are probably right, but what are we supposed to get done?

SCHMIDT: Your ideas are as good as mine, but from the looks of the stuff around here I think we are supposed to build something. My contractor's eye says that these bags of cement and the pile of lumber are meant for building something.

ELIZABETH: Do you really think so, Mr. Schmidt? Build something?

SCHMIDT: As I said, I'm not sure, but my experience would say, "Yes." Let's see if there isn't a blueprint among all this stuff.

ELIZABETH: I can't imagine that I'm supposed to be part of a construction crew. Now really, Mr. Schmidt.

ART: It must be something like that, Ma'am, with all of these tools around here.

ELIZABETH: Well, never in all my life have I been in a situation like this.

DOLLY: Honey, none of us has ever been here before, so let's not worry about it. Here we are and here is all the stuff. I think building something is a swell idea. Maybe we could build a swimming pool—a big one that we could all enjoy. I even have a Bikini I could wear to spice up the scenery a little. The men enjoy it, Mrs. Beacon, even if you don't. What are the chances of building a swimming pool, Smitty?

SCHMIDT: Well, I . . .

LYDIA: I don't want to be misunderstood. I'm not opposed to swimming, nor am I opposed to our building something with all of these materials. But I do want to raise an objection to the construction of a swimming pool. We can build a good many other important things first. Besides, I do not believe we should encourage mixed swimming and immorality through such indecency as a Bikini bathing suit. Surely we have better things to build than that.

JOE: Like a hospital or infirmary, perhaps? Without knowing how long we will be here, it could be very useful. It may save a life someday. I suggest we give it some serious thought.

TERRY: (Wising off) Why not build a billboard for the copper to hide behind to catch innocent victims?

SCHMIDT: That's enough of that, Terry. We are not going to put up with your smart remarks any longer. We will approach this as mature adults or else. (pause.) I think we all realize that we should be doing something. The question is how to decide what.

LYDIA: I think we need that organization that you mentioned.

BETSY: And I move that you become our chairman, Mr. Schmidt, since you seem to know more about building than any of the rest of us.

JOE: I'll second that motion.

SCHMIDT: I don't want to take over this job unless you really want me to. I do think it will help get things done, though, if we organize. Do you want to vote now, or is there another nomination?

DOLLY: Let's get it over with. All in favor of Smitty being our chairman say "Aye." *(They do so.)* Smitty, you're elected.

SCHMIDT: I thank you for this vote of confidence. I think our first order of business ought to be some discussion about our rules and regulations. all set - grab hand

TERRY: I think this is a big, dirty joke and that somebody behind the scenes is laughing his guts out while we try to figure out what is going on. We make fools of ourselves by going in circles and getting nowhere. It's one big mess, it always has been, and it always will be. I vote we forget about the whole thing, throw a party, and not work up a sweat about building something.

ART: Typical teen-ager attitude. *(To Terry)* How long do you think we can last with that kind of garbage, Buster? In most places what you are doing is known as free-loading—gold-bricking. You won't get away with it here, Junior, not if I have anything to say about it.

TERRY: Man, you do talk big for a cop. What do you know about work? If anybody free-loads, it's the cop who rides around in his souped-up car all night and gets paid off all day.

ART: One more crack, Kid, and you and me settle it. I'm not a cop out here and you are just one more smart aleck as far as I'm concerned, and don't forget it.

SCHMIDT: Art, you park yourself over here; Terry, over there. Not another word between you, is that clear? If I'm to be the leader of this group there is going to be some order and respect shown.

ART: Are you going to enforce it, too, Schmidt? You can make your laws and your rules, but who is going to enforce them? If you ask me, we need to begin by building a little respect in punks like this kid here.

ELIZABETH: I agree that we should have some law and order, Mr. Schmidt, and I move that we instate some at once.

LYDIA: And do it right this time. We will not have anyone winking at lawlessness like gambling and drinking *(looks at Dolly)* or worse. I'm for strict laws, stern laws that will keep us safe, secure, and . . . and

TERRY: *(scornfully)* Saved!

LYDIA: I beg your pardon!

HANK: I think he meant "separated." *(Said with a trace of bitterness.)*

LYDIA: I'm afraid I don't understand you, young man, but then I never could understand your kind. Mister chairman, I move we adopt some laws.

SCHMIDT: Can we begin by agreeing that the majority will rule, and that we can work the rest of our rules out from there?

HANK: And what about Joe and me? You add us together and we still don't have any way of counting in this group.

SCHMIDT: You have a voice, Hank, and so does Joe. You can use it, and something tells me you will. I believe there was a motion before the group to develop some rules for ourselves.

TERRY: This is wasting time. I'm sick of the whole mess and bored stiff. If we let these women have their way, we will be having to get permission to comb our hair or blow our noses. You guys can have all the lousy rules you want, but I'm for having some fun while we are still alive. How about a little freedom with these rules—how about a little party? Smitty could be the chief cook and bottlewasher, and his flatfooted friend here could be the bouncer.

ART: *(Jumping on Terry)* I warned you for the last time. That's all I'm taking off of you, Kid.

> *(They begin to fight with Terry scrambling to his feet and pulling a knife from his pocket. LYDIA screams and faints, the two men start for each other as the others move to pull them apart. BETSY is crying as DOLLY tries to comfort her. ELIZABETH is tending LYDIA. SCHMIDT has gained control as ART and TERRY are kept far apart.)*

SCHMIDT: I think it is obvious that something drastic may have to be done. I'm not going to tolerate any more of this from either of you two. If necessary, we can build a jail out of this material and put you both in it. We are going to have order and live peacefully so long as I am chairman of this group. We are not animals to fight at every harsh word. Remember that, Art. And Terry, you will either have to accept responsibility in this group or pay the consequences. *(Pause)* Now, suppose we take some time to cool off, settle down, and think about our plight a little. I declare a recess in our session for fifteen minutes while we think this thing through. Art, I want to see you for a minute.

(*The group disbands with* TERRY, BETSY, *and* DOLLY *in one cluster;* LYDIA *and* ELIZABETH *are still together;* JOE *and* HANK *stroll off to one side together.* ART *meets* SCHMIDT *at C.*)

ART: Don't start lecturing to me about being a hot head. I know all that. But don't blame me if that kid gets hurt unless somebody turns him off. I'm not getting paid here to take that kind of . . .

SCHMIDT: OK, that will do, Art. Just calm down and look at this situation with a little more seriousness—sensibly. This group has got to get busy doing something or they are going to be at each others' throats. They'll make this dispute look like child's play.

ART: I don't follow you.

SCHMIDT: Of course you don't. You have been so concerned about that kid that you have missed the whole issue. People can't stand in suspense like this, not sure of what is going to happen to them, not sure of the danger about them. They can't stand this long. And we have to get busy and build.

ART: Sure, but build what? These people are ready, you heard them say so, but we can't agree on anything. Dolly the Dish wants to swim in her Bikini, Lydia will probably hold out for a temple, and

SCHMIDT: And the truth of the matter is that we need to get a wall up before it's too late.

ART: A wall?

SCHMIDT: Exactly. If you have been listening to the sounds around this place, especially at night, you know that we aren't alone and that there are others around. We know that much.

ART: Oh, I've heard the noises—strange ones, I thought—but I didn't pay much attention to them.

SCHMIDT: Well, you had better start paying attention to them. We don't know what these others are like, what they are up to, and we can't afford to take a chance. It's too risky.

ART: So build a wall, is that it?

SCHMIDT: I had better go talk to that kid before he suspects that I am against him, too. You think it over and see if I'm not right.

ART: Think I'll take a stroll to clear my head. (*Turns.*) Oh yeah, you might strongly suggest to that kid that he lay off if he knows what is good for him. (*Exits same direction as* JOE *and* HANK.)

ELIZABETH: Oh, Mr. Schmidt, have you a moment, please?

SCHMIDT: *(Turning)* Did someone call me?

ELIZABETH: Here, Mr. Schmidt. Mrs. Beacon, I called you. We would like to have a word with you if we could—in private.

SCHMIDT: Surely. *(Joins the ladies.)* Now just what can I do for you two ladies?

ELIZABETH: Lydia and I have been distressed about the way things are going about here. We don't feel the least bit comfortable about it, and we fear the worst might happen if we don't do something soon.

LYDIA: I know that I can't take much more fighting like that. I just can't take it.

SCHMIDT: None of us wants that, I assure you. But do you ladies have any suggestions? We are always happy to work out what we can.

LYDIA: We have been discussing it, but we don't seem to agree. Elizabeth feels we need some sort of community center or club where people can enjoy fine things.

ELIZABETH: Actually, it would be two clubs, Mr. Schmidt. One for those of us who are responsible for the community, and one for . . . well, the others. If you know what I mean. *(Looks in the direction of Dolly.)*

LYDIA: She feels that we might be asking for trouble if we involve everyone in the same group, like those two men, Hank and Joe. They are entitled to their rights, I am sure, but then so are we.

SCHMIDT: I see. I fear that might be a little difficult to accomplish just now, Mrs. Beacon, for we have so few materials and such great needs.

LYDIA: This is what I was saying. Perhaps the clubs can come later if we are here indefinitely. But I do think we can strike a blow right now for decency and goodness. We can erect a church in which we can worship God in the proper way, and teach people to respect his will. We can certainly have some activities at the church to fill the need that Mrs. Beacon feels for fellowship and social life. With restrictions, of course, in keeping with the teachings of the scriptures. But we would certainly separate the sheep from the goats in a hurry if we erected a church where people had to abide by the rules of Christian living in order to be a part of it.

ELIZABETH: I believe it would be a good thing, Lydia, but I am not sure that it is best for us now.

LYDIA: Those young people need to find Christ, Mrs. Beacon, and right away before that Dolly woman completely corrupts them. And we need to see that Joe, the young man from the Orient, becomes a Christian before he goes back so that he can help our missionaries over there.

ELIZABETH: I suppose so, but what will we do with people like Dolly or Terry—or Hank? I don't know that I want them especially for my personal friends, but we cannot just leave them out.

LYDIA: We aren't leaving them out. When they decide to believe as we do, to live respectable lives, they can join the church, too.

SCHMIDT: I appreciate the concern you ladies have shown, but I am afraid that both plans will have to wait. You see, we don't have materials for a church or club and a wall.

LYDIA & ELIZABETH: A wall?

SCHMIDT: There seems to be little doubt in my mind that we have no choice. We must defend ourselves from the dangers that are all about this place with a wall before it is too late.

ELIZABETH: (Seriously) Are these dangers very imminent, Mr. Schmidt?

SCHMIDT: We are not sure, Mrs. Beacon. I know that you have heard the sounds. We only know that there are people all around us, and we are unprotected here without a wall.

ELIZABETH: I had never thought about a wall, though I must admit I have been concerned about our safety at times.

LYDIA: We don't seem to be very safe within, with all this fighting and arguing.

SCHMIDT: That will stop, I assure you, when we begin to work on our wall. There is nothing like a threat from the outside to draw us together.

LYDIA: I suppose you are right in that. It will pull us together. How soon do you plan to begin this work, Mr. Schmidt?

SCHMIDT: It depends on the group's decision. If they vote for it, we will begin at once.

ELIZABETH: You certainly have my support, even though I do like the thought of a community center.

SCHMIDT: Perhaps later, Mrs. Beacon. (Starts to leave.)

ELIZABETH: Perhaps. I do hope so.

LYDIA: Thank you, Mr. Schmidt. It is comforting to know that we have such a dedicated, Christian man at the helm of our group.

SCHMIDT: If you ladies will excuse me, I must talk with young Terry. *(Moves to* TERRY, BETSY, DOLLY.) I hope you will excuse the intrusion, but I feel we need to get some things clear before we assemble again.

DOLLY: Come join us, Smitty. We are having a silent session here.

SCHMIDT: What's that?

TERRY: Betsy refuses to speak to me since the fight, so we aren't saying much over here.

BETSY: He knows full well why I'm not speaking to him, Mr. Schmidt. I have never been so embarrassed in my life. Fighting like a thug or criminal. *(Begins to cry again.)* I'm sorry.

DOLLY: That's all right, honey, if you want to cry, go ahead. I'm sure Smitty has seen women cry before—probably caused a few to cry.

SCHMIDT: That is all behind us now, Betsy, and I think there will be no more fights between Terry and Art. I've talked to Art and he is willing to do all he can to change things. Now I need the same promise from Terry.

TERRY: I don't like cops, never have.

BETSY: Oh why don't you just leave then, Terry. You won't even try.

TERRY: I didn't say I wouldn't try. I just said . . .

DOLLY: We know what you said, Junior. You've said it about a dozen times in the last fifteen minutes.

SCHMIDT: And things are changing—and pretty fast at that. It won't make any difference whether you are a teen-ager and Art a cop—as you put it—if we don't get busy. It won't matter what any of us are.

DOLLY: That's an odd thing to say. What lies behind that remark, Smitty?

SCHMIDT: We can't stand still here, Dolly, stand still and let the world move in and take over. We don't know how long it will be until we are up against it, but we know this, we are flirting with disaster the longer we put off building our wall.

BETSY: We are going to build a wall?

DOLLY: Now that's about the dumbest thing I have ever heard from a grown man. A wall? What are we trying to keep out, bears? This isn't the Middle Ages, Smitty.

SCHMIDT: Nor is it the kingdom on earth, either. You aren't fighting bears today. You are fighting ideas, and people with ideas, and people who can take over whenever they want, unless of course you have . . .

DOLLY: A wall. Same old story.

SCHMIDT: *(Becoming irritated.)* What do you want us to do, roll out a carpet for them to use when they move in and take over? Trouble with people like you is you have a heart of gold and a head full of rocks. You think that by smiling and being nice and loving everybody, you can keep peace and security.

DOLLY: Might be worth a try.

SCHMIDT: Yeah, and in the meantime while you are smiling and throwing kisses at the enemy, they are moving in to take everything we have worked so hard to achieve—to say nothing of what they would do to a sweet young thing like Betsy here.

TERRY: Nobody had better lay a finger on her or they answer to me.

DOLLY: Oh really, now, this is getting absurd—ridiculous—silly.

SCHMIDT: Tell that to Terry when he gets beaten to his knees because he wants to enjoy a little freedom in life—have that party he talked about. Tell it to Elizabeth or Lydia when they are deprived of every possession, every decency. Tell it to . . .

DOLLY: OK, Smitty, OK. Get off the soapbox. Where's my shovel?

SCHMIDT: Terry? What about you? No more trouble, no more fighting?

TERRY: Yeah, no more trouble. If we have to build a wall, we have to build a wall. *(Turns to walk away.)* But it beats me, it really does.

SCHMIDT: Art is out wandering around in that direction. I suggest you try a different route. Or maybe don't go at all. We need to get our session underway. Why don't you round the others up? *(TERRY shrugs his shoulders, changes his direction and begins to gather the group.)*

SCHMIDT: Can you give a shout or a whistle, Terry? Art, Hank, and Joe are out walking somewhere.

TERRY: *(Whistles.)* Let's go, big assembly time! Hurry! Hurry! Get your choice seats. *(All return with JOE and ART in an agitated discussion.)*

SCHMIDT: Very well, let's come to order here and get down to business.

JOE: Before we begin, I would like to know if there is any truth in what Art is telling us. Are we going to build a wall to protect ourselves from the people across the way? Is that true?

SCHMIDT: It has not been voted upon as yet, but it seems from what I can gather that we will probably do that. Why do you ask?

JOE: Is that the only way? Is there no answer? Build a wall? Shut people out?

SCHMIDT: Now that is being a little too strong there, Joe. We are not interested in shutting people out just to shut them out. We are merely trying to take measures to insure our safety, our security.

HANK: Why don't we try negotiations first? Why don't we talk about the matter with these—other people—before we start putting up walls?

JOE: It seems a little rushed to me to judge these people before we know them, to tell them we distrust them from the beginning by building a wall to hide behind. I don't believe it is the right thing to do.

ART: That's not for you to decide. We vote on whether it is right.

HANK: We don't vote on right and wrong. We vote to decide what we will do, but we don't determine right and wrong. It just is.

LYDIA: I'm sure that you men believe what you are saying, but you do not have anything at stake, you have nothing to lose.

JOE: Nothing to lose? We have our lives in this, too.

ELIZABETH: Lydia means you don't have a home and property and a business to lose by trying some idealistic scheme like that.

HANK: Our lives to lose are not the same value, is that it? Our freedom to move among mankind is not of the same worth, is that it?

LYDIA: I don't like the tone of your voice, young man. I try to understand you and to be patient, but I can't seem to do it. You are strange persons—both of you. You don't understand how hard we work to get these things you so lightly put aside. And as for your freedom to "move among mankind," as far as I am concerned you can move out right . . .

SCHMIDT: I believe it would be best for us to entertain a motion at this time about what we shall do with these materials found here. Do I hear a motion?

ELIZABETH: Mr. Chairman, I move that we construct a wall about our little space here to defend ourselves from hostile forces outside, and that we do this with all deliberate speed.

SCHMIDT: Is there a second? (Several others do so.) Very well, is there any more pertinent discussion before we put the question to vote? Art?

ART: I don't have anything to say.

SCHMIDT: Dolly? (*She nods "No."*) Betsy? (*Same*) How about you, Lydia?

LYDIA: Nothing.

SCHMIDT: Terry?

TERRY: Still seems odd to me.

SCHMIDT: But you have no objection to raise? (*Terry nods "No."*) Elizabeth? (*Same*) Hank?

HANK: It just can't be right that our primary purpose in this place with all these materials is to build a wall to close us in and others out.

SCHMIDT: (*Directed*) But in the interest of harmony within our group so that everyone has a place of security inside—all of us here—you will go along with the majority? (HANK *looks, then nods "Yes."*) Joe?

JOE: I have nothing to say.

SCHMIDT: Then are we ready for the vote? (*Several nod "Yes."*) All those in favor then of building the wall let it be known by saying "aye." (*Nearly all do so.*) And those opposed. (*No response.*) Then it is a wall we shall build—and at once.

Act 2

> (*Fadeout on the scene which comes back up revealing the group at work on the wall. Music helps the transition. Missing are* TERRY *and* SCHMIDT *at the beginning.*)

DOLLY: (*Mixing mortar*) Let's declare a coffee break! I'm about to break into two equally tired parts. (*She stops her work.*)

BETSY: I agree. This is harder work than I imagined.

ELIZABETH: My dear youngster, if you think it is hard for a young body like yours to do this work, you should hear the protests that my own is making. If only we could have paid to have this work done.

ART: You ladies knocking off for coffee already? (*Joins them.*)

LYDIA: I should say we are. It doesn't seem quite right to me that we should have to work as hard as you men, or as long.

ART: Sorry, but that is the way it is. You have as much at stake in this matter as any one of us men. You will have to admit that we do look after you ladies somewhat.

HANK: (*Joining the group*) Somewhat? The way my back feels it seems I have personally carried every stone used for this wall.

ELIZABETH: You certainly have worked very hard, Hank—you and Joe. I don't know how we could have done it without you two.

HANK: Thank you, Mrs. Beacon.

JOE: Those are kind words that make the ache somewhat better.

ELIZABETH: We have all worked very hard, and I feel that we are indeed fortunate in having Mr. Schmidt and Art here to provide the brains for our project, and you two fine men to provide the strength and brawn.

LYDIA: Yes, we must confess that our wall, like much we have, is due to the hard work of such men as Joe and Hank. I think it is good when each man takes his rightful place to make a community work.

JOE: *(Offended)* Rightful place? I am not sure . . .

HANK: *(Extending a hand to stop Joe.)* We probably need to get back to the job and let these ladies have their coffee break, don't you think, Joe. *(After tense silence the three men finally return to the wall.)*

LYDIA: Did I say something wrong? I must say that was a strange reaction for someone to make when you are complimenting them on doing good work. I just will never understand those people.

BETSY: I think they accepted your compliment but it didn't stop with kind words, I'm afraid.

DOLLY: You managed to toss in a little sociology, prejudice, and personal opinion along with the compliment, honey. I think it was their reaction to this that you noticed; it wasn't hard to catch.

LYDIA: What do you mean by that remark? Are you trying to say something derogatory about me?

DOLLY: Call it whatever you like. I only said that your prejudices were showing through in your compliment.

LYDIA: I take offense at that remark. As a Christian I believe I know right from wrong, good from bad and when someone of your —your moral fibre speaks about prejudice, I think I have a right to be offended. I don't recall seeing you set any example—good example, that is—for anyone around here. I only hope that we can undo some of the influence you have already had on this young lady here and her boy friend.

DOLLY: *(Anger mounting)* I have a good mind to punch you in your pious, self-righteous nose. Nobody, Christian or otherwise, is going to get away with some . . .

ELIZABETH: Oh dear, not you two. We don't have time to argue and fight. *(Calling)* Mr. Schmidt, Art, someone come quickly. Mr. Schmidt, Art.

LYDIA: I believe I am entitled to my opinion, and if the occasion comes for me to state it, I will.

DOLLY: Your opinion is poison, and smells to high heaven. If you are in any way a representative of religion, then I can assure you that you will never have to worry about me corrupting your church. I wouldn't set foot . . .

SCHMIDT: *(Running on the stage as the others gather, save* TERRY.*)* Now what is it?

ELIZABETH: I'm afraid we have a serious difference of opinion between these two ladies, Mr. Schmidt, and we just can't afford any more trouble now, can we?

SCHMIDT: Ladies, please, I know that this work is very hard for you and that you are very tired, but we just cannot fall apart now. We are so nearly finished with our work that we will have to hold out only a little more. Now what is the dispute?

LYDIA: She is making accusations about me that I don't care to repeat.

DOLLY: But you would gladly repeat what you have said about me. You would delight in that, wouldn't you?

SCHMIDT: All right, coffee break is over, and so is the argument. I order that the two of you refrain from another word to each other the rest of the time we are building the wall. *(To the group.)* And to all of you, let me plead with you to hold out a little longer. The wall is nearly completed and we can rest afterwards knowing that we are safe from all attack, and we can pursue our other interests in peace and happiness. So let's get back to the building of the wall before . . .

TERRY: *(Running on the stage)* Hey, wait, wait a minute, just a minute. *(Pants for his breath).* Before you leave, we had better get ready—to meet a visitor—a guy coming this way.

ART: We may be putting our wall to the test sooner than we had expected.

LYDIA: A visitor coming here? What on earth does he want?

ELIZABETH: What did he look like? Was he foreign? What was he wearing?

JOE: Was he alone, or did he have someone with him?

HANK: Did you talk to him? What did he say he wanted?

TERRY: Hey! One question at a time.

SCHMIDT: All right, everyone calm down. *(Moves toward* TERRY.*)* Now, suppose we let Terry tell us what he knows.

TERRY: *(Still panting.)* All I know is that this guy is coming this way. He suddenly came walking along the road where I was looking for some more rocks for the wall. He asked me if he was headed in the right direction to get here. I told him yes, then took off to warn you that he was coming.

SCHMIDT: Well, what did he look like? Can't you tell us something about him?

TERRY: He looks—well, like the rest of us—sort of normal. He is friendly enough, I guess. I didn't stick around too long to see just what he had in mind. All I know is that he was coming from the other direction and this meant he was a stranger to be dealt with.

ART: This could be bad for us—a person coming to see how our wall stands, to see how weak we are right now to defend ourselves.

LYDIA: Do you suppose he is a spy or something like that?

JOE: Maybe he is coming to negotiate with us.

HANK: He could be a friend as well as a foe. I think we ought to give him the benefit of the doubt at least.

ELIZABETH: Yes, but if we are wrong and he is out to do us harm, then it may be too late. Before he gets here, I think I will excuse myself to put a few things out of sight. You just never know when someone may come to take your possessions. *(She exits.)*

ART: I think I will go and get my gun just in case. It doesn't hurt to have something around to protect ourselves in case he is up to no good. *(Exits.)*

BETSY: I'm not sure I want to be here when he comes—not right at first. I'm a little afraid of strangers anyway. May I be excused, Mr. Schmidt? *(Exits.)*

SCHMIDT: As long as we are not sure what he is up to, I suppose we should keep ourselves scattered. But someone needs to meet him and talk with him. Hank, you and Joe, why don't you greet him for us all?

JOE: Why us—all of a sudden—I mean? I thought we were the brawn here, not the brains.

LYDIA: I'm not so sure how it would look either, if you know what I mean, for this person to have his first impression of us here.

HANK: Don't worry about that; Joe and I will be out gathering more rock, using our strength. Perhaps you can represent us

LYDIA: I don't think it would be proper for a lady to be the one to greet him. No, I think I will go find Elizabeth. Perhaps we can seek God's help in this difficult matter. *(Exits.)*

TERRY: Difficult? What's so difficult about it? All we have to do is be here when this guy comes. I don't get it. There are nine of us and one of him. Doesn't seem like such a bad risk to me.

SCHMIDT: But we can't take any chances. We have to consider all the possible pitfalls. And you are too young, inexperienced, and hot tempered to greet this man. I suggest you go find Art and stay with him. *(TERRY exits.)*

DOLLY: Well, I suppose I should make myself scarce, too. Smitty, do make a good impression on this man, will you? He may be a nice man and we don't want to drive any of them away, if you follow me.

SCHMIDT: You won't have to worry about me driving anybody away, my dear. Just be sure you don't do it yourself.

DOLLY: Me? I may never see him at this rate, so never fear.

SCHMIDT: But I think it would be good for you to see him first. Sort of a community hostess if you know what I mean.

DOLLY: Community hostess? What sort of silly idea is this, anyway?

SCHMIDT: No, I'm serious. As the elected leader of this group I don't think it would be best for me to expose myself too soon to this man until we know what he wants. It is like having a diplomat to lay the groundwork for you, Dolly. And that is the task I want you to perform. So please get yourself ready; he will surely be appearing any moment. I'll retire to my office and wait until you are sure of his purpose in coming before I greet him officially. *(Exits.)*

DOLLY: Well, how do you like that! Community hostess! What a laugh! *(Calling to SCHMIDT.)* Maybe you had better bolt the door, too, until I give you the pass word that it's safe to come out.

BUILDER: *(Entering)* Hello there.

DOLLY: *(Startled)* Hello, yourself. *(Looks at him for a moment.)* Hello, and welcome to the friendliest place on earth. We specialize in greeting strangers, taking them to our hearts. You will find all the big wheels around here either in hiding, or hiding their priceless jewels until we are sure you are a "good guy." In a little while you may be approached by some of them, not with a key to the city, exactly, but a little routine search and questions to check you out. We see a lot of detective films here, you know. I'm the official committee of one to extend to you the right hand of brotherhood and love and say, "Welcome." The name is Dolly. I'm a woman with something of a past, a limited present, and a hopeless future. That ought to do it. Now, who are you?

BUILDER: Thank you for the welcome, such as it is. But I do understand how some of your people could be a little apprehensive.

DOLLY: Well, that is a generous way to put it. I'd say they are scared stiff myself. But then you are more considerate, as a guest ought to be. What brings you here, if we can get right down to the point?

BUILDER: I have been sent really. I'm a builder, too. Something like the rest of you here, and I am coming with the blueprints. But I see you have already begun work.

DOLLY: Great! We are nearly finished with the job and you arrive with the blueprints. I'm afraid it may be a little too late, unless of course we guessed it right the first time.

BUILDER: From the looks of things you are building a wall instead.

DOLLY: Instead? That's what I was afraid you might say. Well, what were we supposed to make out of all this mess around here. We didn't find any suggestions lying around among the cement sacks.

BUILDER: But it is not intended to be a mess, not really.

DOLLY: According to whom? You?

BUILDER: According to me, yes, but also the one who put you here in the first place.

DOLLY: Now that's the guy I want to talk to. I didn't exactly ask to be tossed here, but here I am. And I have a few questions to ask —like just why? What are the chances of you getting me an appointment?

BUILDER: It is not as complicated as all that, Dolly. Not really. But we can speak of that later. What concerns me now is how we can change the way things are going here with the building project.

DOLLY: Now that isn't going to be so easy—not after all the effort we have put into this wall. I think maybe you had best try some other approach—for your own sake, if you follow me. The chief might not care much for any changes.

BUILDER: The chief?

DOLLY: Yeah, ole Smitty, Mr. Schmidt, that is. He will doubt that you are on the level. *(Pause)* Come to think of it, how do I know you are on the level? Here I stand talking to you like I have known you all my life.

BUILDER: You don't know if I am on the level, yet. You will have to take my word for it that I'm here representing the one who is behind all of this enterprise. But you will see for yourself, surely.

DOLLY: Think so? Perhaps. But let's get the others out here to help decide. *(Calls.)* Hey Terry, Terry! Get your whistle to working and call the brave citizens together to meet this man. (TERRY *appears.)*

TERRY: Is it all right?

DOLLY: He hasn't even raised his voice to me. So get them rounded up. (TERRY *whistles and begins to call to the others.)* You could run for president as far as I'm concerned, but then I'm not much judge of people. *(Suddenly)* By the way, are you a politician?

BUILDER: No, I'm not. Why do you ask?

DOLLY: Just wondering, that's all. The last guy I trusted like this was running after more than just an office. I decided not to get out on a limb like that again.

SCHMIDT: *(Walking officially to the* BUILDER.*)* How do you do, Sir. Mr. Schmidt, C. A. Schmidt, chairman of this group. Sorry that we were not on hand to greet you, but official business detained us.

BUILDER: Yes, I understand well how pressing matters can get in a case like this.

SCHMIDT: *(As the others now gather about the* BUILDER.*)* And of course we felt we needed to know something more about you and your intentions.

ELIZABETH: And your background.

ART: We are peace-loving people here, and we aim to keep it that way. We aren't interested in welcoming any trouble into our group, if you know what I mean.

BUILDER: I assure you that I have not come to bring trouble—not of that sort. I actually came for a different purpose. I thought I might be able to shed a little light on the problem you have here.

TERRY: Problem? What problem?

BUILDER: The problem of how to use these materials you find all about you.

JOE: That seems to be cared for already. We are building a wall with it.

BUILDER: So I understand. *(Silence.)*

LYDIA: But you don't approve.

BUILDER: It's not exactly whether or not I approve; it is whether or not this was the intention.

HANK: Intention—whose intention?

DOLLY: He says he comes from the one who originated all of this stuff anyway.

SCHMIDT: The one who originated all of this? Who? How do we know this? What authority do you have to prove this statement? What is your authorization?

BUILDER: I'm afraid that I only know what his will is on this matter and I do have his blueprint for the job that is to be done with the materials.

ART: And that blueprint calls for what? Or is it too soon to ask that question?

BUILDER: No, I think you ought to ask it.

SCHMIDT: Then what does the original blueprint call for, if it's not the wall?

BUILDER: A bridge.

ALL OF THEM: Bridge?

BUILDER: Yes, a bridge—a bridge between this place and those other places all about you.

ELIZABETH: Not a wall?

BUILDER: Not a wall, not a wall at all. We have far too many of them as it is. We need more bridges—bridges over which the traffic can flow both ways, bridges that take you from here to other places and bring other places to you here.

ART: And so we open ourselves up to attack. We not only tear down our walls, but we build bridges over which they can come and defeat us.

BUILDER: Why do you fear these people? Are you not really the same—part of the same family of human beings?

HANK: A fair question. I think that it deserves some consideration.

LYDIA: You would think that. I'm not sure I go along with this at all. I can't see any sense in our tearing down our walls when we are not sure who this man is. How do we know that he comes from the originator behind all of this?

ART: How do we know he isn't coming from the other side, and just trying to talk us into trusting them so they can take over?

BUILDER: You don't know. You just have to trust me, have faith in me, and see that I'm telling you the truth. You will not accomplish anything that the originator had in mind by concentrating all your efforts on building a wall. You need to divert this energy toward building bridges, I tell you—bridges that bring you face to face with other persons like yourself who are hiding now behind walls, behind fears. They need to know of your interest in their well-being, their lives. They need to feel your love flowing toward them to reassure them that they can come out of hiding, tear down their walls and live as the originator had in mind. Bridges will do this better than walls.

TERRY: But what if they don't tear down their walls, what if they storm us, take us over—just because we fell for your silly dreams?

ELIZABETH: I believe that it is taking a dreadful chance with so much here to safeguard—to say nothing of our very lives.

BUILDER: But your lives are meaningless if all you do is hide them behind walls that shut you in, behind fears that chain you down. You live in darkness this way. Let me bring a little light into your lives. Trust me and you will see what I mean.

JOE: You make it sound so simple, but that is a bigger gamble than you think. Trust you, you say. What if we do and discover that we have been tricked, then what?

BETSY: What if you are a spy, like somebody said a little while ago?

ART: (*Beginning to become agitated.*) Yeah, what if you are a spy? I don't like the phony way you come walking in here without any papers or authorization—just your word for it.

LYDIA: It's too dangerous to just fall in behind you, tear down our walls.

HANK: The risk is more than you have a right to ask us to make.

SCHMIDT: Now, give the man a chance. Let's not judge him too fast.

BUILDER: What I am urging you to do I am doing myself. I have come here to help you build a bridge. I am building a bridge as I come to you—a bridge between you and the originator of this project.

ELIZABETH: That is what you tell us, but how do we know you are telling us the truth?

ART: Why should we believe you any more than any other man who happens to walk into our group?

TERRY: I think we need some proof that you are who you say you are.

BUILDER: You must believe me. If you do not tear down the walls and come out into the free sunshine to live, if you do not crawl out from under your fears and walk like men, then it may be too late and you will find only dismal days ahead of you.

HANK: Is that a threat of some kind? Are you telling us that if we don't tear down this wall, you are going to do something to us?

BUILDER: Not I. No, I am not threatening you. I am only telling you the truth. You will do it to yourselves.

JOE: We have fought hard to build good will among our group. We are not perfect, but we certainly are not living in dismal ways, either.

BUILDER: But you will. You will. Bridges that allow men to move about freely as intended—these are the answer, not walls. You must tear them down.

ART: No! I will not tear them down. And nobody around here is going to force us to tear them down. We are going to finish our walls and we are going to live securely behind them. And any of you who agree with me, tell this character so.

LYDIA: I certainly do not intend to let our walls be torn down. How do we know he doesn't have a whole army of his kind waiting to pounce on us the minute we destroy our wall? We destroy our wall and we destroy ourselves.

BUILDER: No, you are wrong.

ELIZABETH: Wrong, are we? Wrong! And what do you know about what is right and wrong for us. You wander in here without any identification and expect to take over. Mr. Schmidt is our leader, not you, and I defy you to touch a single stone in our wall.

BUILDER: I come to you as a friend, as one who builds, too. I do not come as a foe.

HANK: That is what you say, but what do you do to prove it? You ask us to destroy our defenses, to expose ourselves to your mad scheme. I say you are worse than a foe, for you are a wolf in sheep's clothing.

BETSY: (Growing hysterical) A spy, a spy! You are a spy just as I said.

SCHMIDT: Now wait a minute, wait a minute. You must not be too quick to condemn this man.

ART: He is condemning himself. We didn't ask him to come here. He appears, tries to trick us, and doesn't succeed. He condemns himself.

TERRY: But I think we ought to finish the job and let his friends know what we think of spies—of their little tricks that are designed to destroy us.

BUILDER: I tell you good will prevail over evil, men are meant to walk bridges, not hide behind walls. Walls must be torn down, barriers must be lowered, and bridges of good will and concern must be put in their place if man is ever to walk in true freedom.

ART: You mean if men from the other side are ever to walk freely into our community and take it. That's what you mean.

SCHMIDT: If only you had some proof that you could be trusted. But you have nothing, and we can only doubt your word because it is madness to do otherwise. I fear what may become of you if you stay here.

DOLLY: Why don't you leave now while you can? These people don't want to hear you.

BUILDER: But they must. They have no choice. It is my way or death.

JOE: Death? Whose death—our death or your death? You don't scare me talking big like that. As a matter of fact, you only make me want to fight all the more, to show your friends what we think of their plot.

ART: *(Moving toward the* BUILDER*)* I think we have taken enough from this man. He has tried every way he can to trick us, to talk us into mass suicide. I say let's get rid of him.

BUILDER: If you would only listen to me, believe me.

HANK: I say let's get rid of him, dispose of him. He's dangerous.

SCHMIDT: Let's do this with law and order. No violence.

BUILDER: I am a friend. I came as one, and I shall leave as one. *(Turns to leave.)*

ART: *(Jumping toward him, grabbing him, and whirling him around.)* No, you don't. You don't walk out of here like that. You don't get away to inform others of our defenses.

TERRY: Let's give them a little example of our strength. Let's make an example out of this stooge of theirs. Let's get him.

> *(At this point the organ begins rumbling, the shouts build up among the group, who are busy hitting the* BUILDER *with whatever they can find. They shout and scream, "Kill him" and "Get rid of him" as the music builds louder and*

louder. They drag the BUILDER *to the place on the stage where the cross is lying. He is placed on it, it is quickly raised and swung around with the backside to the audience after a brief moment. The organ has hit a peak at the precise moment that the cross is raised, as* BETSY *screams,* LYDIA *drops in a faint, and everyone shrinks back in horror of what they have done. Only* DOLLY *remains standing in the light. After a long silence she speaks.)*

DOLLY: But we just have to learn; we just have to learn. We can't go on crucifying the Truth forever.

(She stands motionless as the curtain falls.)

WED 6-9

9-3-

TUE F S

(WED AOO

$.3